LAWS WE NEED TO KNOW

Understanding Rules and Programs

For Persons with Mental Illness

By Baron L. Miller J.D.

Printed in the United States of America

First Printing, 2020

Paperback: ISBN 978-1-7347712-0-6

Ebook:ISBN 978-1-7347712-2-0

Baron L. Miller
1388 Sutter St. Suite 710
SAN FRANCISCO, CA 94109

www.baronmillerlaw.com

ABOUT THE AUTHOR

Baron L. Miller has practiced law in San Francisco, California continuously since 1973. He is a frequent writer and lecturer on legal issues faced by family members of mentally ill persons, and he has been advising and assisting clients and other attorneys on these issues for decades. He has an adult daughter with schizophrenia, and he is a long-time NAMI member and advocate. www.baronmillerlaw.com

ACKNOWLEDGMENTS

I thank the following persons for their assistance in producing this book:

My wife, Nancy Keyes, for her constant love and support.

My daughter, Izra Miller, for modeling resolve, and for providing inspiration.

My sister, Probate Paralegal Lynn M. Nightingale, for her review of content pertinent to probate procedures, and her comments and suggestions, and for over decades having taught me much of probate procedures (among other things).

My friend, Attorney Dale G. Major, for his review of content pertinent to criminal procedures, and his comments and suggestions.

My friend, Steve Snyder of CLEARWEB.io, for his expert design formats, content and copy reviews, ideas, publishing and creative prowess, understanding, and spirit.

My friend, Netty Kahan, retired professional editor, for her editing comments and suggestions.

All persons suffering from mental illness, and their families and friends, who courageously deal with its immense challenges, and who help me do the same.

Baron L. Miller
San Francisco, California
August, 2020

TABLE OF CONTENTS

PREFACE

People afflicted with severe mental illnesses so serious and debilitating as to impair their abilities to care for themselves need assistance and support from others. I think that those persons who provide that needed help will benefit from a resource that explains pertinent laws and legal procedures, and is available at their fingertips. This book is written primarily for them.

This book is also written for those persons who suffer from severe mental illnesses and who are frequently referred to as "high functioning," *i.e.*, those who are able to care for themselves in many important ways and perform many daily tasks without assistance. I think they too will beneficially use the information here.

This book is also written for the lawyers and social workers and doctors and nurses and everyone else who find themselves in need of a reference source for information concerning severe mental illness.

A few notes on labels used in this book:

Persons who suffer from severe mental illnesses are usually consumers of mental health services and are frequently referred to by providers of services and others as *consumers*. It is as *Consumers* that they will be referred to here.

Those who emotionally, financially, and practically support Consumers without receiving compensation – such as family members and friends – are referred to here as *Supporters*.

One more definition: all Consumers and Supporters, and all persons who interact with them, will be collectively referred to as *the Mental Health Community*.

There are numerous laws and government assistance programs and government protection procedures that exist for Consumers. While they provide varying degrees of benefit, all of them are valuable. The value can only exist, however, if Consumers are able to access and use them. The laws establishing programs, and the rules and processes which control them, are often complex, sometimes too much so for most of us to fully understand. A purpose of this book is to provide enough information and explanation to enable the Mental Health Community to understand the laws and the government programs and processes so that we can help Consumers and Supporters to the fullest extent possible.

In addition to comprehending laws and programs, an important purpose of this book is to educate Supporters on how to provide care after we, the Supporters, due to death or disability, are unable to provide care ourselves. Estate planning for families with mentally ill members is just as important as anything else we do.

Still another purpose of this book is to explain the rights of Consumers and the protections available for Supporters when criminal offenses and other liability-incurring conduct occurs.

This book tries to list and describe the most prominent laws and programs pertinent to mental illness, i.e., the ones we are most likely to encounter, to explain how they work, and to offer tips on making them work effectively. Footnoted references to applicable laws are presented when it appears that this would benefit readers by enabling them to obtain additional information which would assist them in understanding the law. This book will not replace a social worker or a lawyer when one is needed; but likely it will reduce the number of times one will be needed.

One thing this book does not try to do is to be an exhaustive listing or explanation of all of the laws and regulations applicable to those who suffer mental illnesses or to their Supporters. There are a multitude of laws pertinent to Consumers, and many are lengthy and complex. There are myriad laws, rules and procedures which govern institutions that Consumers might be interacting with at different points in their lives, such as hospitals, jails, schools, and courts. Inclusion of all of these laws is not possible or practical, and only those of them which are directly pertinent to issues presented in this book are set out and explained.

The United States is a nation of fifty states, with each state divided into numerous counties, and the counties divided into even more cities. There are federal, state, county, and city laws and programs, all of which affect the Mental Health Community. My legal knowledge is basically confined to the laws of the United States and of the State of California, and when specific laws and procedures are presented in this book, it will be those.

California law is divided into various *codes*, each of which contains laws pertaining to a similar subject matter. For example, there is a Vehicle Code which contains most of the laws pertaining to operating motor vehicles. When a code is listed in this book, unless otherwise specified, it is a California code. Each state has its own laws affecting Consumers, and I have found that they are often similar to California's, both in their content and applicability, but not necessarily the same in all ways. So, while a resident of, *e.g.*, Florida can rely on the information in this book in general, it is important to recognize that a specific procedure or law of California as presented in this book will not necessarily exist in Florida. Specific laws, procedures, and the applicability of them in Florida can be ascertained only by accessing Florida law, which usually means contacting a lawyer familiar with Florida law.

One final caveat: Laws change daily. Chances are that the vast majority of laws and legal procedures cited in this book will remain constant for many years. But not all will, and it is necessary to be aware of this, and to understand that what is presented is current now, but that some of the laws and procedures described here will surely change.

A note on gender usage: The Mental Health Community, being a randomly formed group, is approximately one-half female and one-half male. It has been traditional to use *he* and *his* when referring to members of such groups, although there is no evident justification for this use. Possibly joining a new tradition, *she* and *her* will be used in this book wherever singular personal pronouns are needed for someone unidentified by gender.[1]

I sometimes say that when my child was diagnosed with schizophrenia in 1990, I knew next to nothing about mental illness, and since then, like most caring parents of mentally ill persons, I have become an involuntary expert on the subject. The expert part is intended as an ironic overstatement of the awareness that I, as a parent, have acquired, but certainly I have been compelled to obtain a lot of knowledge about mental illness and the laws pertaining to it. Almost daily I dispense this knowledge to the Mental Health Community, and I will continue to do so. At the same time, I hope that my advice and the advice of other attorneys in this field will become complementary to this book, and *vice versa*, and that the Mental Health Community will be able to readily look up and beneficially use the information that is provided here.

---

[1] Certainly, no offense is intended toward those who prefer using the pronouns, *they* and *their*. As *they,* and *their* are plural pronouns, they are not traditionally grammatical when referring to an individual, so *she* and *her* will be used here.

CHAPTER 1

COMMUNICATIONS WITH AUTHORITIES AND INSTITUTIONS

Introduction

When a Consumer needs to communicate with persons who have authority over situations affecting her, such as government workers, financial institutions, medical providers, police, teachers, and social workers, she faces no legal obstacles to doing so. There are things that might impede her communications with authorities, such as the communicative abilities of the authorities and of the Consumer, and the ability and desire of the authorities to devote the time needed for the communication. But there are no legal prohibitions to her communications.

It is often not as easy for a Supporter to communicate with authorities when she needs to do so. As Supporters, we are usually ready and eager to communicate freely with authorities, but authorities won't always communicate with us. Frequently authorities cite the law as their reason.

Our nation is governed by laws, and the foremost of these laws – the United States Constitution – protects everyone's right to privacy and to freedom from unwanted intrusion. The United States Congress and fifty state legislatures have enacted laws to ensure that these privacy and freedom rights are honored and respected. This reflects the high value placed on individual rights in this country. The enactment of these laws is decent and principled and important, and should make one proud to be an American. There are times, though, when one of these laws — that which prevents medical authorities from providing needed information about a patient to a Supporter without the patient's authorization — can cause unintended problems.

The idea behind this law is that communications between a patient and her medical providers are private, and that private communications should be protected. This law accomplishes that, since, in other than exceptional situations, it enables a patient to prevent disclosure of information about her to another person simply by refusing to authorize it. The problem, as we know, is that requiring a patient to authorize disclosure is not always a good thing.

There are times when authorities need to receive pertinent facts about a Consumer, and the Consumer is unable to adequately provide them. There are also times when a Supporter needs information about a Consumer who refuses or is unable to share it with the Supporter. In order to help a Consumer, Supporters and authorities need to share information with each other. Most medical providers recognize the benefit and need of obtaining information from those persons who help a patient, and the benefit and need of giving information to them. But if a patient will not authorize disclosure, then it is common for these authorities to refuse to communicate information to us.

There are some medical providers who, while they may not be willing to violate a Consumer's right of privacy and their own legal duties, can and will dispense information to Supporters as needed. As discussed below, they find a way to do this.

There are also exceptional situations where medical providers are exempt from respecting a right of privacy, and in those situations, it can be said that they are not only allowed to disclose information, but that they are required to do so. These situations arise, as discussed below, when medical providers have concluded that a disclosure of confidential information is in the best interests of a patient because the patient lacks the ability to consent or object to disclosure, due to the patient being incapacitated, or due to the emergency nature of the situation.

Absent any such exceptional situation, Supporters have no right to obtain information from authorities without the existence of a legal authorization. Often the best we can hope to do is to persuade a medical provider to listen in order to get important information, and to respond to our questions with hypothetical answers.

Below is a synopsis of some laws and legal procedures, knowledge of which provides Supporters with the maximum opportunity of having meaningful communications with persons exercising authority over a Consumer.

When a Consumer is a Minor

Each state has its own laws regarding communications about minors between parents and guardians on the one hand and school, medical, and governmental employees on the other. All of these laws exempt parents and guardians from privacy considerations except in specific and exceptional circumstances. So, unless there is something extraordinary which prevents it, such as a child abuse investigation, a parent or guardian will be able to obtain needed information about her minor child, and communicate information back to the authorities.

What constitutes a minor varies from state to state – it is somewhere between the age of 18 (as it is in California) and the age of 21. There is also a legal concept of emancipation which enables a minor to be treated as an adult and which would affect situations in these infrequent cases. For the vast majority of instances though, parents and guardians of minors are going to have an unimpeded ability to communicate with authorities regarding their minor children.

When a Consumer is an Adult

Usually most of one's life is spent not as a minor, but as an adult. So most communications with authorities will occur when a Consumer is an adult, when a Supporter has no right to obtain information from authorities without a legal authorization from the Consumer or a court order. Authorization can arise in a number of ways, and without it free communications can be dependent on those persons a Supporter is dealing with. Let's look at the potential situations.

When There is No Authorization

The Requirements and the Exceptions

If there is no authorization from a Consumer or a conservator or an authorized agent (see below), then the law requires authorities to respect the privacy belonging to those they directly serve, and usually to refuse requests for information from Supporters.

Without an authorization some authorities refuse to communicate at all with Supporters, even just to receive information from us. Some medical providers won't acknowledge that a Consumer is their patient, or that she is in their institution, apparently reasoning that this information would violate the Consumer's privacy. Some won't even return phone calls, possibly believing that this courtesy would violate privacy. And sometimes when they do return calls, they might as well not have done so. So long as a Consumer is communicating adequately with her medical providers this can be tolerable, if barely so.

A big problem arises when due to a confused state of mind a Consumer resists assistance and refuses to authorize authorities to communicate with Supporters. When there is a crucial need for us to communicate with authorities, being ignored is not acceptable, and it is unlikely that we will be patriotically assessing the situation as encompassing sacred Constitutional rights. Instead we will be justifiably infuriated by a Consumer being allowed to self-destruct because she lacks the current mental ability to allow those who care about her, and who regularly provide care for her, to help her not self-destruct. Someday the law might better reflect the correctness of our feelings. But as of now, if a Consumer refuses to authorize authorities to give information to a Supporter, then there is a good chance the authorities will conclude they have a legal obligation to deny the Supporter the needed information.

Many doctors and nurses and staff who cannot obtain an authorization from a Consumer allowing them to disclose information to Supporters will tell us our input is valued, and they will encourage us to talk to them. The communication might only go one way, but certainly this is better than no communication, although it is still pretty much guaranteed to frustrate us. After all, we are not voyeurs, we are not trolls, we are not looking to exploit anyone's personal information, we have no malevolent intent. Quite the opposite, we are trying to help someone we care about, someone who can't help herself.

In the midst of our exasperation, it is important for us to keep in mind that almost surely medical professionals are not trying to irritate us. A physician might want to share information with her patient's Supporter, recognizing how it could help her treat her patient, and how it could assist the Supporter in helping the patient, and how it might ease a Supporter's emotional burden to learn more about the patient's condition. But so long as privacy laws do not distinguish between persons whose thinking is rational and persons for whom thinking has become irrational, personal medical information of one not consistently rational is often going to be deemed private and confidential, and absent an express authorization from a Consumer, it will not be shared with a Supporter.

Many medical professionals in this situation encourage Supporters to give them pertinent information about a Consumer and will express their desire to communicate with us. Some medical professionals will explain to Supporters the processes and procedures that are employed in the situation a Consumer is in at that time, and in effect offer us theoretical responses, *i.e.*, the medical provider will say what would occur if a hypothetical patient were in a situation similar to the Consumer's situation. Sometimes it can be helpful for Supporters to suggest this approach to the medical professionals. It won't work for all – surely, we can't expect a medical professional who is refusing to acknowledge a relationship with a real Consumer to acknowledge that a Supporter might have an interest in some hypothetical Consumer. But we don't know it won't work, so when necessary it is best to give the authorities the opportunity to do this by making the suggestion.

There is an important exception to the privacy rules prohibiting disclosure of a patient's information to non-authorized persons. Contained in *Regulations*[2] enacted by the United States Department of Health and Human Services for the purpose of informing and guiding medical practitioners on how to comply with privacy laws, this rule allows disclosure of medical information to a relative or friend of a patient when disclosure is in the best interests of a patient and 1) the patient lacks the capacity to make health care decisions, or 2) it is an emergency situation, or 3) the patient is not present.[3] This regulation uses the qualifiers, *incapacity*, *emergency situation*, and *not present* to refer to situations where the patient is unable to agree or object to disclosure. If a medical professional were to conclude that her patient's thinking is impaired to the point where the patient doesn't understand the benefits

---

[2] Regulations are types of laws which are established by governmental departments to govern situations over which the department has jurisdiction and the power to regulate. So, *e.g.*, the U.S. Department of Health and Human Services has jurisdiction over medical providers, and can and does establish Regulations governing the provision of medical services.
[3] 45 Code of Federal Regulations, section 164.510(b)(3), (2014)

of allowing disclosure, and the impairment causes the patient to imagine negative effects of disclosure which in reality do not exist, then the medical professional could conclude that her patient lacks capacity to agree to or object to disclosure. If the medical professional then concluded that disclosure of confidential information was in the patient's best interests, she could legally disclose it.

While this regulation provides reasonable hope to Supporters, the standard for disclosure is still a very high one. A medical provider might be faced with a patient in the middle of a psychotic episode where contradictory and fantastical ideas are expressed as reality. The provider might see this as a situation where the patient is likely incapacitated to such a degree that the patient cannot make a reasonable decision about disclosure, and that, therefore, disclosure is in the patient's best interests. The provider might also conclude that the patient is "not present" due to incapacity, and that disclosure is therefore permissible under that allowable standard. But the provider might still recognize the possibility that despite the patient's condition, the patient has a rational reason for refusing to allow disclosure.[4]

Some medical providers see their job somewhat narrowly – as treating a patient, not a patient's friend or family – and they may not believe that the friend or family can assist in the treatment process. Frequently medical professionals don't know the relationship between a Consumer and her Supporter well enough to know if the Consumer's objections, seemingly irrational, might be indeed rational, or *vice versa*. Based on a chance that the Consumer is rational in her refusal to authorize disclosure, the provider might conclude that she cannot disclose information without the Consumer's authorization.

When we are enraged over a forced inability to help our Consumer, we might say that a medical provider who can't separate a patient's reality from her fantasy when it is obvious to everyone else is a worthless medical provider. And maybe she is. But from this provider's

---

[4] As someone famously said, paranoiacs also have real enemies.

point of view, her patients have privacy rights and may have good reasons for not waiving them, even if they are unable to clearly state those reasons. It is not the medical professional who is so much at fault here as it is the wording of the law. The regulations do not define "not present," nor do they say how "incapacity" to make a reasonable decision about disclosure is determined. Medical providers are being required to use their own judgment and to determine by themselves whether an unauthorized disclosure is the best way to treat a patient.

An irrational person might believe that a Supporter is harming her, and say this to her medical providers. It is hoped that providers can distinguish between their patients' realties and delusions, but it isn't always easy. Sometimes providers believe their patients' fantasies are real, or simply just don't know if they are.

We are appropriately exasperated when we are not allowed to help our Consumers, but it usually isn't fair to blame a self-protective medical provider. She may justifiably fear what would happen to her if she made an unauthorized disclosure and the patient later objected and was able to establish that she was harmed as a result of that disclosure. A change in the law that would enable disclosure where a provider believes it would be more likely than not beneficial, and would exempt providers from future liability, would be helpful.

Incapacity

Most Supporters would be pleased if a Consumer were deemed to be incapacitated and found to be not present, so that the Supporter could obtain necessary information about the Consumer. But medical providers might see things differently. Before a medical provider would conclude that a Consumer is incapacitated to the extent that sharing confidential information is allowed, the provider must believe that she has the authority to determine the Consumer's capacity. It should not be shocking to anyone if a provider were to conclude that a determination of incapacity can only be made by a court. There is no requirement in the law for this, but neither does the law say just who does have the authority to determine incapacity. Requiring a court order is a safe approach for a provider to take.

There is a California law that says everyone is presumed to have capacity to make decisions and to be responsible for them.[5] This law exists for the purpose of a court establishing someone's incapacity, and it allows the rebuttal of this presumption with evidence of incapacity. A physician unwilling to make her own determination of incapacity might well cite this law to a Supporter who is seeking confidential information about a Consumer. The physician would in effect be saying, "You need to petition a court, produce the evidence of incapacity, and obtain a court order. Then I will obey the court order and disclose the information." Of course, this is not what we want to hear. We want information, not litigation. A Supporter's best response might be something like, "A court order of incapacity would be based on your (the physician's) findings and opinion. Better to make the determination of incapacity now, and let your patient later petition a court to try to establish her capacity if she actually wants to, at which point the evidence of incapacity would surely prevail anyway." But if a Supporter is dealing with a physician who wants no possibility of future problems and sees the way to accomplish that goal is by disclosing information only with a court order, then the disclosure is not going to be made without one.

California law says what factors should be weighed in determining incapacity.[6] Included are the presence of, the absence of, or the impairment of, the following: alertness, attention, memory, comprehension, communicativeness, reasoning, planning, organization, hallucinations, delusions, uncontrollable thoughts, and modulation of mood appropriate to circumstances.

We can cite laws and argue their application to our situation for as long as anyone will listen to us, but the reality here is that if a Supporter finds herself trying to persuade a medical provider that

---

[5] Probate Code section 810.
[6] Probate Code section 811.

disclosure is allowed due to incapacity, then unless the provider was confused by her obligations, the Supporter will likely be unsuccessful. At which point the most the Supporter is going to be able to accomplish is to get hypothetical responses to her questions.

Emergency

A physician who does not want to take responsibility for determining incapacity might be more inclined to divulge information based on the emergency nature of the situation. Medical personnel deal with emergencies, and generally they don't need to reflect on what might constitute one. The law says, and physicians understand well, that an emergency situation is one of urgency, one where the person in authority concludes that a patient will suffer immediate harm absent some otherwise outlawed communication. As said above, this emergency situation will render an authority exempt from violating the right of privacy. It should be expected that a medical provider will treat a situation as an emergency if a patient is a danger to herself and the provider needs a Supporter's help to remove or reduce that danger. But other than to reduce the risk of a potential suicide, a medical provider might be unwilling to find an emergency which would allow her to disclose otherwise unauthorized information.

A medical provider also has the authority to disclose medical information if she believes it is necessary to prevent or reduce a serious and imminent threat to the health or safety not only of a Consumer, but to members of the public. In fact, a medical provider not only has the authority, she also has the legal duty to disclose information in order to prevent harm to another.[7] Where one (with or without a mental illness) has expressed what appears to be a serious desire to harm someone, those in authority who have this information must notify the potential victim of the threatened harm. And if the threat is of imminent harm, coupled with an apparent ability to carry it out, the threat itself might constitute a crime and thus would be reportable to the police. This rule

---

[7] *Tarasoff v. Regents of University of California* (1976) 17 C.3d 425.

is certainly significant, but it will not help a Supporter gain knowledge of a Consumer's situation unless it is the Supporter who has been threatened, and even then, it might only provide the Supporter with the fact of the threat, and not necessarily with information concerning the Consumer's treatment.

Summary of Requirements and Exceptions

In a situation where the symptoms of a Consumer's illness prevent her from recognizing the effects of her illness and the need for assistance from her Supporters, a preposterous situation is created where patients lacking rationality are being treated the same as those who have no impediments to good decision-making. By preventing Supporters from communicating with authorities, a Consumer's symptoms often sabotage her needed care. The law readily recognizes that infants lack the ability to make their own medical decisions. An adult in the midst of a psychotic episode which prevents her from comprehending her illness and its needed treatment has no more ability to help herself than an infant does. Why then should she be taken care of any differently than an infant would be? It is an empty platitude if not outright nonsense to say that as a society we are respecting individual rights when in fact we are simply allowing individuals to self-destruct because they don't realize they are self-destructing. But until we change it, we must deal with the law as it is, not as we would want it to be.

Sometimes a medical provider recognizes the futility of slavishly adhering to a law that might be wonderful in other settings but makes no sense under the circumstances. This medical provider might be looking for a way to help when an incapacitated Consumer will not authorize a needed disclosure of information. If the medical provider recognizes that because of a Supporter's involvement in a Consumer's care it is in the Consumer's best interests to disclose information to the Supporter, that medical provider might want to be able to make a determination that the Consumer is incapacitated or "not present" so that the provider can then voluntarily disclose information to a Supporter. These situations are not always clear, and medical providers do rightly concern themselves with the potential liability of violating a patient's rights. Sometimes, if a medical provider will tell us nothing else, she will tell us what happens in similar situations with similar patients as this does not technically or directly violate the patient's privacy. It is always worth trying to help reluctant medical providers reach a point where they will provide information to us.

Types of Authorizations

Institutional Consent Forms

Hospitals and medical offices frequently maintain their own authorization forms, and they might require that their own forms be used, *i.e.*, that a needed authorization be contained in that form. This would require a Consumer to be in a rational frame of mind at the time the form is presented to her so that she will sign it and give a Supporter authority to communicate with those persons who would help her. That presentation is usually done when a Supporter is not there to offer advice to the Consumer as to why it would be beneficial for her to sign it. Which means the result is sometimes a matter not of reason or logic, but of the Consumer lacking the ability to understand the need for a disclosure of information, and having no one there to help her understand it.

Powers of Attorney

A lawyer is also called an *attorney*, but a power of attorney is not a reference to a lawyer. This use of the word actually means *agent*. An agent is one with the power to act for another. That is what a power of attorney is – a power given to another person – usually called the *agent*, sometimes called the *attorney-in-fact* – which enables her to act on behalf of the person giving the power (called the *principal*), and to legally bind the principal by those acts. A power of attorney is created by signing a document spelling out the powers given to an agent who is designated as such in the document.

The powers given in a power of attorney can be for various things. Some powers of attorney are limited to specific matters, and some are unlimited in the powers given. Depending on how it is worded, a power of attorney might become void upon the principal losing capacity, or it might not become effective until the principal does lose capacity. Sometimes powers of attorney can be made *durable*, which means that the powers are effective immediately and they endure, *i.e.*, they remain in full force and effect, should the principal become incapacitated. Durable powers of attorney are the most commonly used, certainly for future planning, as they will cover a situation where a principal cannot otherwise help herself, *i.e.*, when she becomes incapacitated.

The two most common types of durable powers of attorney are a general financial power of attorney and a medical power of attorney.

Durable Power of Attorney for Financial Matters

An adult can give another adult a financial power of attorney. It consists of a written designation of another to serve as an agent to make financial decisions and to transact financial business for the person giving the power, who is, again, called the principal. It can be made durable, which as mentioned above means it remains in effect if the principal becomes incapacitated. It could also be made a *springing* power, which means it won't go into effect until the principal becomes incapacitated. The problem with a springing power is establishing incapacity, *i.e.*, who will establish it and under what standard. Durable avoids that, and is therefore usually better, as the agent is already able to act and doesn't need to establish her need to act.

It is advisable for a Supporter to have a Consumer execute a durable power of attorney for finances when the Consumer is willing and able, and then to file it away safely until needed. These powers of attorney are revocable, but absent a revocation, financial institutions and governmental agencies generally respect them, and these powers of attorney will enable us to take care of business in ways we never could otherwise.

Power of attorney forms can be obtained online or in a stationary store, but because of the options available in the forms and the importance of getting them right, it is recommended that an attorney be hired, preferably to draft the document and have it executed, but at least to discuss it and the available powers that can be contained in it. In addition to these powers of attorney requiring choices to be made by the person signing them, they need to be executed in conformance with the law of the state where they are being signed. An attorney would be expected to do this correctly, and her doing it should be relatively inexpensive. It is certainly not a requirement that an attorney be involved, but if it is done incorrectly it will likely be invalid and of no use.

Durable Power of Attorney for Medical Decisions

Just as she can do with her finances, an adult can also give another adult the power to make medical decisions. The power to make medical decisions necessarily includes the ability to communicate with medical providers. It is also advisable to get one of these powers of attorney executed by a Consumer when she is willing and able, as it can allow communications to take place with medical providers, even years later. This power is also revocable, and if a Consumer were to refuse to sign an in-house authorization presented to her by a medical institution then the institution would likely conclude that this power has been effectively revoked. But this relatively simple document may well be what enables Supporters to communicate with medical personnel, and so should be obtained from a Consumer when it can be. It too can and should be made durable. Forms are available online and in stationary stores, and often in physicians' offices. If the form being signed is not that of a medical institution or provider, then it would be best to have it drafted or reviewed by an attorney who would explain the options and oversee execution of it and ensure that it is done correctly.

Conservatorship

There is a type of court proceeding where a court will bestow authority on one to make decisions for another who lacks the capacity to make her own decisions. This proceeding is alternately referred to as a *conservatorship* or a *guardianship*. Usually it is a conservatorship that is established for an adult who lacks capacity, and a guardianship for a minor. The proceeding for an adult will be referred to here as a conservatorship.

In California there are two types of conservatorships – a Lanterman-Petris-Short Act (LPS) conservatorship (see Chapter 2) and a probate conservatorship (see Chapters 7 and 10). Other states have LPS-type conservatorships, although they are called something other than an LPS which is a name unique to California. Once either of these types of conservatorships is ordered by a court and put in place, it may enable a Supporter to communicate with authorities.

An LPS conservatorship is initiated by a county for the predominant purpose of hospitalizing a Consumer against her will. It is usually the county which is designated the *conservator* (the operator of the conservatorship) and is given the power to involuntarily hospitalize someone, but the conservatorship can be established in a way that this power is given to or shared with a Supporter. A Probate conservatorship exists for all situations and needs except involuntary hospitalization, and if a Supporter is made the conservator then she will have the authority to do many things, including communicating with authorities.

Both types of conservatorships are complex, labor-intensive for attorneys and courts, and expensive. A conservatorship is always a large undertaking, and often it is only obtained after a court battle with a Consumer. It should be considered a drastic measure to be used only in situations where no other option exists to accomplish that which needs to be accomplished. It would depend on the specific situation but trying to establish a conservatorship solely for the purpose of attaining the ability to communicate with persons who have authority over a

Consumer might be unwise. However, a conservatorship can give the conservator that power, and there are situations where an inability to communicate is not a temporary occurrence, and where those in authority will not cooperate or communicate with a Supporter in any fashion whatsoever. In these situations, it might be necessary to establish a conservatorship as the only way to help a Consumer.

It must be understood that while a conservatorship will give the conservator the power to communicate with persons in authority, there is no reason to believe it will change a recalcitrant Consumer into a willing or eager collaborator. In fact, as a conservatorship might be seen by a Consumer as nothing more than an attempt to take away her autonomy, it might harden a Consumer's resistance to receiving assistance. Neither will it necessarily change the perspective of a person in authority who has decided she is wasting her time dealing with a Supporter. The idea of instituting conservatorship proceedings is something to be reviewed at length with one's attorney, and never to be entered into lightly, nor with unreasonably high expectations.

Conclusion

There will be encounters with authorities who will not disclose information to us without an authorization from a Consumer, and if none, then without a court order. We can prepare for this by obtaining the authorization beforehand with a power of attorney, or we could seek a court order in a conservatorship proceeding at the time the privacy laws are being invoked against us. And we should always try to help an authority understand her legal ability to communicate with us even without a power of attorney or court order.

There will be times when no matter what we do, we are going to be unable to get authorities to communicate with us. When that occurs perhaps the best that can be done is to do nothing that will make the situation worse. Future contact with resistant authorities is possible or even likely, and we do not want to make those contacts more difficult or more nonproductive than they might otherwise be.

Laws are needed that more clearly define the circumstances under which medical professionals can disclose private information to another without a formal authorization. The laws need to specifically allow disclosure when the medical professional concludes it is more likely than not that disclosure will help the patient, and they need to generally exempt medical professionals from liability if it is later established that a patient had a good reason for not waiving her privacy rights.

What is also needed are hospitals with rules established to deal immediately with a situation where there is no express authorization. It is understandable that a single medical professional might not be willing to take the risk of improperly disclosing confidential information. So when this issue arises, as it does with some frequency in psychiatric units, hospitals could have a review process set up where other medical providers are apprised of the issue and weigh in on the response to it. If, for example, *two* psychiatrists are consulted, and both agree that disclosure would be helpful and the refusal of the patient to authorize it is due to the patient's irrational mental state, that should certainly have greater value than if just one concluded this.

For the time being it is our job to inform medical professionals of their right, and possibly their obligation, to disclose information when a Consumer is incapacitated and therefore unable to understand her need to authorize disclosure. We can try to persuade these authorities that a Consumer's irrational refusal to accept help, by itself, establishes her incapacity, resulting in the Consumer's best interests being furthered by disclosure.[8] We need to make it clear to an authority who, after all, concludes she cannot divulge specific information about a Consumer, that there is nothing to prevent her from saying what generally happens

---

[8] Persuasion strategies are discussed in Chapter 13.

in like situations with similar patients. Lastly, if everything else fails, our job is to lick our wounds and prepare for the next fight.

CHAPTER 2

HOSPITALIZATION

Introduction

Many, if not most Consumers, experience hospital stays. Frequently the first hospitalization is an involuntary one which results in an initial diagnosis. Future hospitalizations can occur when medications stop working, or aren't taken, or there is some major stressor that induces an aggravation of depression or psychosis. Because a hospitalization means treatment and safety, it is often sought after by Supporters.

Hospitalizations can be voluntary, where a Consumer is admitted to a hospital at her own request, or they can be involuntary, where a Consumer is admitted and held against her will. In order to obtain legal authorization for a hospital hold on a Consumer against her will for longer than 72 hours it is necessary to obtain a court order after a hearing, and for a longer hold it is necessary to obtain a court-ordered conservatorship. There is also a process existing in some counties within California and in other states where a person can be found by a court to be dangerous to others based on her illness and past acts of violence, after which she can be held against her will if she refuses to cooperate with mental health professionals in her prescribed treatment.

Voluntary vs. Involuntary Hospitalization

A person with mental illness can ask her doctor to admit her to a psychiatric unit in a hospital, or in the alternative she can walk into a hospital emergency department where there is a psychiatric unit and ask to be admitted. In these situations, if her condition is deemed by her doctor or by an emergency room physician to require hospitalization, and if there is room for her in a psychiatric unit, and if she has the financial means to pay for it, either through a public benefit, private insurance, or personal wealth, then she will receive the requested admission. This is called a "voluntary admission." If the Consumer is a minor, then it would be her parents or other legal guardian who have the authority to request a voluntary admission, and she would need to consent to it; otherwise it would require an involuntary admission process (see below).

When a Consumer is deemed by medical professionals to need hospitalization, and she refuses to cooperate in the process or lacks the financial means to pay for hospitalization, then she can only be hospitalized through the involuntary admission process. This process is known in California as a "5150 admission," or simply a "5150."[9] In addition to being used as an adjective, 5150 is frequently used also as a verb, as in, "are you going to 5150 her?" and as an adverb, as in, "she is being 5150ed." 5150 means that one is being admitted to a locked psychiatric unit against her will – an involuntarily admission. It is also referred to as an "LPS hold."[10] In other states a 5150 admission or LPS hold is referred to in other ways, but the procedures are substantially similar.

The 5150 procedure usually starts with the police. If the police believe someone has a mental disorder which results in her being a

---

[9] This name is derived from the specific law that provides for the involuntary admission procedure. That law is found at Sections 5150 *et seq* of the Welfare and Institutions Code.

[10] Sections 5150 *et seq* of the Welfare and Institutions Code comprise the Lanterman-Petris-Short Act, named after the three legislators who proposed and promoted its passage. It has become known by its acronym, *LPS*.

danger to herself or others, or which results in her being "gravely disabled," they can transport her to a mental health facility for a potential 5150 admission.

One is deemed to constitute a danger to herself or others when she expresses a desire and intention to commit imminent harm, or if there is other evidence of that desire and intention. To be deemed a danger to oneself, overt statements or actions regarding suicide are not necessarily required; if one's disregard for her own safety is at the point where a serious physical injury to her is imminent, *i.e.*, she has actually placed herself in physical jeopardy, that is sufficient to qualify as being a danger to herself.

In order for someone to be gravely disabled, she must be found to be suffering from a mental disorder which renders her unable to provide for her basic personal needs for food, clothing, or shelter. Courts of Appeal (courts that hear appeals from trial courts, as opposed to trial courts, which hold trials) have the power to interpret statutory language, and their interpretations become part of the law on the subject being interpreted. The actual words used by a California appellate court to define "gravely disabled" are: "...the person, due to mental disorder, is incapacitated or rendered unable to carry out the transactions necessary for survival or otherwise provide for her basic needs of food, clothing, or shelter."[11] This same court ruled that evidence of a third party's willingness to assist the patient must be considered, as a person would not reach the quality of being gravely disabled if she could survive safely with the assistance of a willing third party. A third party's willingness to assist, however, is not by itself sufficient; there must also be an actual ability on the part of the third party to assist and an actual ability on the part of the Consumer to accept assistance.

---

[11] *Conservatorship of Smith* (1986) 187 Cal. App. 3d 903, 909. The court did not define its phrase, "the transactions necessary for survival," but did refer to the party in the case as being able to avoid "malnutrition, overexposure, or any other sign of poor health or neglect," so presumably those are the transactions.

A 5150 hold means the person subject to the hold can be kept in a locked psychiatric facility for up to 72 hours. If deemed an emergency, antipsychotic medication can be involuntarily administered; otherwise a court hearing must be held on whether medication can be given to a patient against her will (see below). While the police can bring someone to a mental health facility, in order to place the person on a 5150 hold only the mental health professionals at the facility can make the finding that she is a danger to herself or others, or is gravely disabled.

Minors are subject to being held under a procedure similar to a 5150, although it is technically not a 5150 admission as there is a separate set of code sections which apply to minors. The process is almost the same, the major difference being that a minor must be held in a facility that is specifically operated only for minors.

The ability of mental health professionals to place a Consumer on a 5150 hold is necessarily limited by the resources available. The intolerable and obvious reality of present-day life is that there are far more people in need of 5150 holds than there are beds in mental health facilities to keep them. Anyone in a large city with a temperate climate virtually anywhere in the United States need only walk down a busy street any time of day to see the large numbers of people who obviously cannot adequately care for themselves and who quite obviously need psychiatric help. However, the scarcity of hospital capacity need not deter us. When Supporters recognize the possible need for a 5150 hold, we should contact the police and/or the Consumer's treating psychiatrist as a first step in the process.

Sometimes a Consumer can pull herself together and display rationality for a short period of time, frequently inopportune times such as when the police arrive or when being interviewed at a mental health facility. It is helpful when interacting with the police and with the mental health professionals if a Supporter is able to give them a concise summary of the Consumer's recent behavior which is believed to necessitate a 5150 so that the full situation is understood. Often those with the authority to place a Consumer on a 5150 hold need our assistance to more fully understand the situation.

If the mental health professionals at the facility where a Consumer is on a 5150 hold believe she will need more than 72 hours of inpatient treatment, then they can sign a certification which states that the patient requires up to an additional 14 days of detention and treatment. A hearing – called a Certification Review Hearing – must be held within 4 days of this certification, and evidence must be presented at this hearing to support the certification. This is a "5250" procedure.[12]

The hearing officer who presides at a certification review hearing is selected by the county where the psychiatric facility is located. She can be a judge, an attorney, a certified law student, or a medical or psychological professional. The hearing normally takes place at the county psychiatric facility where the Consumer is being held. The person who is held against her will is entitled to be present at the hearing, and to have an appointed patients' rights advocate represent her at the hearing. The patients' rights advocate is not usually an attorney, but she is someone familiar with the applicable law, and her job is to represent the patient in the patient's efforts to accomplish release or avoid medication. The hearing is private (closed to the public), and Supporters are allowed there only if we are going to be witnesses who are testifying – either to the need for further hospitalization or the opposite – or if the Consumer does not object to our presence. The issue to be determined is the same as the one that prompts a 5150 admission to begin with: whether the patient is a danger to herself or others, or gravely disabled.

If after the certification review hearing a Consumer's need for a hold in excess of 72 hours is ordered by the hearing officer, the Consumer has a right to petition a court for release based on a lack of dangerousness or grave disability. This procedure is known as a Habeas

---

[12] This procedure is also named for the Welfare and Institutions Code section which provides for it.

Corpus proceeding, and will result in another hearing, this one before a judicial officer – a judge or court commissioner (essentially an assistant judge given the powers of a judge) – where the same or additional facts will be presented to the judicial officer. At a Habeas Corpus hearing a Consumer is entitled to a court-appointed attorney, which would be at the Consumer's own cost if she has the financial ability to pay for it.

If the certification for up to 14 days of additional treatment is upheld, and if treatment beyond those additional 14 days is deemed needed, then the procedure employed to hold the Consumer will depend on the reason for it.

Where after an initial hold of 72 hours and an additional hold of 14 days the county believes the Consumer is still a danger to herself, then it can certify a need for another 14-day hold.[13] Upon this certification of self-danger being made, the Consumer can be held for up to 14 more days. There is no right to a certification review hearing, although the Consumer does have a right to petition for Habeas Corpus and thus obtain a court review that way.

Where after an initial hold of 72 hours and an additional hold of 14 days the county believes the Consumer is a danger to others, then the county can petition the court for an order of confinement for an additional 180 days of treatment.[14] The Consumer has a right to a court hearing, and a jury if she desires it, and appointment of an attorney to represent her. Again, the cost of the attorney would be borne by the Consumer if she has the ability to pay for it. Additional 180 day periods of confinement for treatment can be ordered by the court after the same procedure is employed.

Where, after an initial hold of 72 hours and an additional hold of 14 days, the county believes the Consumer is gravely disabled, then in some counties it can certify the need for a hold for up to an additional

---

[13] Welfare and Institutions Code sections 5260 *et seq.*
[14] Welfare and Institutions Code sections 5300 *et seq.*

30 days. This procedure only exists in counties that have provided specifically for it.[15] As part of this process, a certification review hearing must be held, unless the Consumer requests a jury trial, as she is entitled to one. The same procedures are employed as in the other certification review hearings and court hearings mentioned above.

To hold a Consumer against her will beyond these time periods requires either 1) a new 5150 hold being initiated, or 2) in the case of a gravely disabled Consumer, the filing of a petition for an LPS conservatorship (as explained below).

If the treatment plan includes the use of anti-psychotic medication, and if the patient does not consent to it, then it can only be administered if there is an emergency situation or if there is a court order. If a Consumer refuses to take anti-psychotic medication and there is no emergency, then a petition would need to be filed by the mental health provider and a court hearing without a jury would then take place on the issue of whether the patient lacks capacity to refuse medication. This hearing is referred to as a *capacity hearing* (formerly and still sometimes called a *Riese hearing*[16]). It will take place in the medical facility where the Consumer is being held. The Consumer is entitled to appointment of a patient rights advocate or an attorney to represent her at the capacity hearing, which will be conducted by a Superior Court judge, commissioner, or appointed hearing officer.

LPS Conservatorship

There is a type of conservatorship which gives a conservator the authority to place the conservatee in a locked psychiatric unit. It is

---

[15] Welfare and Institutions Code sections 5270.10 *et seq.*
[16] It took its name from the appellate court case which required the hearing – *Riese v. St. Mary's Hosp. & Med. Ctr.* (1987) 209 CA3d 1303 – before the legislature amended the Welfare and Institutions Code so that the code itself now provides for it. See Welfare and Institutions Code sections 5332, 5333 and 5334.

known as an LPS conservatorship.[17] Its purpose is to obtain authority to place a person who is deemed gravely disabled in a mental health treatment facility when she is unable to freely consent to the placement, and to require the administration of psychotropic medication to her. It can be established after the procedures listed above, or in a criminal proceeding without these procedures ever being instituted.[18]

In a conservatorship, the Consumer is called the conservatee, and the person ordered by the court to administer (operate) the conservatorship is called the conservator. It is the conservator who will possess the authority to place the conservatee in a locked mental health treatment facility, where medication may be administered if the conservatee agrees to receive it or if a court orders it after a capacity hearing (see above).

An LPS conservatorship is initiated by the county of the hospital where the patient has been admitted. It is done by the county filing a petition with the court on the recommendation of the mental health professionals treating the patient. Minors can be the subject of a petition. The petition will state who is being sought to be the court-ordered conservator. If a family member is qualified and has expressed a willingness to serve, and there is not a resistance from the patient that would disturb the process, the petition may ask for the appointment of this person as conservator.[19] Otherwise the petition will ask for the Public Guardian's office of the county to be appointed as conservator; this is the most common occurrence. Infrequently a county and a family

---

[17] The law which provides for this type of conservatorship is found at sections 5150 *et seq* of the Welfare and Institutions Code. See footnote 2. These conservatorships have become known as *LPS conservatorships*.

[18] Chapter 3 contains a description of LPS conservatorships established after a criminal court referral.

[19] Problems can arise when a patient will not authorize the mental health professionals to disclose information to a family member who would be an appropriate conservator. See Chapter 1. No confidentiality constraints are necessarily placed on communications between mental health professionals and county officials who would investigate and petition for the conservatorship, nor generally on communications between non-medical county officials and family members. Different counties handle these confidentiality issues in different ways, and it is not feasible to try to list all of the ways.

member will be appointed co-conservators. An LPS conservatorship is most commonly a personal conservatorship of the conservatee and not a conservator of her assets, but if the conservatee has assets that need protection, and she does not have a probate conservator[20] to protect them, then the court can also order an LPS conservatorship of the conservatee's assets – called a conservatorship of the estate – in order to protect those assets.

An LPS conservatorship will be ordered only after a hearing, except where evidence of a need for an immediate conservatorship is presented to a court, in which case a temporary conservatorship may be ordered without a hearing. A temporary conservatorship can last for up to 30 days so as to allow time for the hearing and for further orders.

Again, an LPS conservatorship will only be ordered if there is a court finding that the proposed conservatee is gravely disabled. Again, in order to be found gravely disabled, one must suffer from a mental disorder that incapacitates her, or that renders her unable to carry out the transactions necessary for survival or otherwise provide for her basic needs of food, clothing, or shelter.

As part of the conservatorship process a proposed conservatee is entitled to legal representation, and if she cannot afford an attorney then one will be appointed for her. If she desires a jury trial, she is entitled to one. She also has the right to insist on confidentiality of the proceedings.

An LPS conservatorship is for a one-year period and can be renewed by petition and hearing annually. It is also the county that has the sole authority to file this renewal petition. The conservatee has the same rights on a renewal petition as on the initial petition, including appointment of an attorney if she cannot afford to hire one, and a jury trial. Significantly, a court could determine without a trial that a conservatee lacks mental capacity to make the decision to request a jury

---

[20] See Chapter 7 for an explanation of a probate conservatorship.

trial. After a conservatorship has been established, the conservatee retains various rights, including the right to petition the court regarding the appropriateness of a particular placement.

A problem that frequently occurs is a refusal of a county to institute an LPS conservatorship when it is evident to a Supporter that one is needed. This may be due to bad judgment on the part of county officials, but more likely it is due to budget constraints. The reality is that many if not most counties lack the resources to conserve and hospitalize the many persons who actually do fall within the category of persons for whom an LPS conservatorship properly exists. There is an informal triage process that occurs, and it results in many persons who need help not getting help. Again, a walk through the streets of a good-sized city enables us to see this problem in action, where persons who seem to fall within the definition of being gravely disabled are living lives of homelessness and despair.

Another problem is the narrow limitation on what will allow an LPS conservatorship to be ordered. Many Consumers who do not fit into the definition of gravely disabled are crucially in need of medical care and will not obtain it on their own. The problem was presented perhaps most cogently and presciently by Justice Donald King, a renowned 20th century trial and appellate court judge, in his concurring opinion in Conservatorship of Smith:[21]

> Every citizen in California will surely be horrified to learn that the only possible legal recourse where a nondangerous mentally ill person continuously engages in unlawful conduct, but can provide food, clothing and shelter for herself, is to repeatedly place that person in jail for disturbing the peace. More should be expected from a civilized society.... A great many seriously disturbed men and women now inhabit the downtown areas of our major cities, too mentally ill to avoid running afoul of the law but not ill enough to be treated under an LPS conservatorship. If civil commitment with treatment provided

---

[21] *Conservatorship of Smith* (1986) 187 Cal. App. 3d 903 at pg. 911.

to cope with mental illness is inappropriate for such persons, incarceration in county jail is certainly even less appropriate....

Access to needed medical care is a basic human right and is of particular importance to those whose very illnesses cause them to refuse care. Perhaps this is the proper time for the Legislature to reexamine public policy toward the mentally ill and ensure the provision of essential medical treatment to those who so desperately, both literally and figuratively, cry out for it.

Without some change in public policy, the phenomenon of dramatically increasing numbers of the mentally ill living on the streets and in the doorways of our major cities, and paying periodic visits to our county jails, will all too certainly become an integral part of contemporary society.

There is a procedure in the LPS Act which allows a court to order an appraisal of an individual to determine if she qualifies for an LPS conservatorship. It is begun with a petition filed by a family member or friend. The court is empowered to order an appraisal, but the court cannot order the conservatorship unless the county will then petition for it. The problem with this procedure is that often it is as evident to the county as to anyone else that an LPS conservatorship is needed, and the issue is not that the county refuses to make an evaluation but that the county refuses to petition for an LPS conservatorship. It is quite a regrettable reality of our society that we do not establish and fund the resources to house and treat sick people. Obtaining a court order requiring a county to evaluate a Consumer may be an empty gesture, since the county is not necessarily required to take any particular action after doing the evaluation.

Assisted Outpatient Treatment

A law allowing assisted outpatient treatment, sometimes referred to by the acronym AOT, and frequently called Laura's Law in California (and modelled on what is called Kendra's Law in New York), was enacted by the California Legislature to deal with the situation where the mental condition of a person with a mental illness is deteriorating, but she has not yet reached the level of impairment required for a 5150 admission. This law allows, but does not require, individual counties to enact their own laws which mandate assisted outpatient treatment for such persons. Some counties have done so. The law only applies to a limited class of persons with deteriorating conditions, specifically those who 1) have a current history of hospitalizations or incarcerations due to mental illness, 2) have been provided with and have refused an opportunity to voluntarily participate in treatment, and 3) have a history of not complying with treatment.

The assisted outpatient treatment, which may consist of counseling, medication, and other programs, must be court-ordered. If the individual does not comply with the treatment plan, then the court can order her involuntarily hospitalized so that treatment can occur. The idea behind AOT is to pay attention to the history of one's illness, to prevent acts of violence against oneself or others, and to prevent one from becoming gravely disabled, by treating the illness before it deteriorates to a point of violence.

Again, AOT does not automatically apply to everyone in the state of California. Instead, it applies only to those applicable persons in a county which has enacted the AOT law that state law has allowed it to enact.

Conclusion

Repeated hospitalizations for Consumers are not uncommon. They are frequently welcome, at least to Supporters, as an opportunity for a Consumer to receive more intensive diagnosis and treatment, and to enable her to be in a safe place. Sometimes it seems like there is no one with authority who cares enough about a Consumer to actually do anything to help her, while at other times there are authorities who recognize her needs and do what they can, including the initiation of the involuntary hospitalization process. Supporters should be familiar with the laws and procedures surrounding hospitalizations so that we can take advantage of them when available, and so we can cooperate in the procedures to the extent possible. We need to be ready for all of it.

CHAPTER 3

ARRESTS AND CRIMINAL JUSTICE

Introduction

It is an unhappy reality that persons with severe mental illnesses that go untreated, or whose medication regimen is not working, sometimes are accused of committing crimes. This chapter generally explains the California criminal justice process for adults, and how it applies to persons with mental illness. The process in other states and in the federal system is substantially similar. For those looking for more detailed information, it can be found in numerous places. One good place is the Criminal Rules which comprise Title 4. of the California Rules of Court.

Classification of Crimes

California law lists and defines all of the various kinds of criminal activity which the state has the power to control,[22] and specifies the potential

---

[22] There are some crimes which due to the United States Constitution or federal statutes are only federal crimes. *E.G.,* treason is solely a federal crime, chargeable only in federal court, not in a state court. However, there may well be elements of such a federal crime which also constitute a state crime. And, *e.g.,* if one organizes a militia for the purpose of overthrowing the United States government by force, that could result in a federal charge of treason. But if the militia steals guns to further its cause, and practices shooting them in areas where such practice is not allowed, or uses the guns to threaten or otherwise harm others, state crimes have been committed and can be charged by the state.

punishment for each listed crime. Most of California's laws concerning crimes and punishment can be found in the Penal Code. Other California codes containing crimes and their punishments are the Health and Safety Code, Welfare and Institutions Code, and Vehicle Code.

All California crimes are classified as being one of three types: an infraction, a misdemeanor, or a felony. The classification is dependent on the punishment prescribed for a violation. An infraction is a crime which is punishable by something other than incarceration, *i.e.*, the potential punishment is a fine and/or community service. A misdemeanor is a crime which is punishable by incarceration for up to one year in a county jail. A felony is a crime which is punishable by incarceration for more than one year, which must occur in a state prison and not in a county jail. Misdemeanors and felonies may also carry fines, community service, and probation (explained below under the heading of Punishment) as possible punishments.

In addition to the punishment provided for each class of crime, each class may have its own court procedures, as explained below.

Policing and Prosecution

There are various law enforcement offices in California that police communities and other areas, with the majority of law enforcement officers working in city police departments, county sheriff departments, and in the California Highway Patrol.

In each California county there is an Office of the District Attorney which prosecutes criminal cases.

Arrest and Release

The power to arrest depends on the type of crime believed to have been committed.

A peace officer, *e.g.*, a police officer, a sheriff's deputy, or a highway patrolperson, who believes one has committed an infraction, can issue a citation to that person, requiring a court appearance.

A peace officer can arrest a person who commits a misdemeanor in the officer's presence. If not committed in her presence, then usually an arrest warrant must be issued by a court before an arrest can be made for a misdemeanor. There is also a "citizen's arrest," where one who has witnessed a crime being committed announces to a peace officer that she is placing the accused under arrest and asks the peace officer to take the accused into custody. It is frequently the victim of a crime who makes a citizen's arrest of the crime's perpetrator.

An arrest can be made by a peace officer for a felony if the officer has cause to believe the arrested person committed the felony, without the crime having occurred in the officer's presence and without a warrant and without a citizen's arrest.

Generally, one who is arrested has a right to be released pending trial if she pays or arranges for payment of bail. Bail is a sum of money deposited with the court for the purpose of insuring the appearance of the person arrested at all court hearings. A nonappearance would result in the bail being forfeited to the county and an arrest warrant being issued by the court. An original arrest warrant will fix the amount of the bail, and if there is no warrant, then bail will be in an amount set in a local court bail schedule. The idea behind a release on bail is that it provides a monetary incentive to an arrested person to appear in court at her hearings.[23]

---

[23] There is a movement afoot to reform the bail system, and to make release pending trial available to those who lack funds for bail. Presently the bail system described here is the one still employed in most places.

If a case is begun by the issuance of a citation, the court has discretion whether to require bail.

If one arrested cannot afford the bail, then she can apply to a bail bondsman which has already qualified with the court as the agent of a recognized and financially viable insurance company. The bail bondsman can post a bail bond in lieu of actual bail money. When using a bondsman, there is generally a fee of 10% of the bail amount which must be paid to the bondsman before the bail bond is posted, and this is paid to the bondsman and is nonrefundable. If there is a nonappearance, then the bonding company that posted the bail bond will be responsible to pay the amount of the bond to the court.

If the amount of bail is not affordable, then the person arrested can apply to the court for a reduced amount, or for a release without paying bail (known as being released on her own recognizance, or O.R.). O.R. will be granted where circumstances are such that there is a strong expectation that the person arrested will appear in court as required. Factors weighing in on the side of an arrested person in her O.R. determination are her residence in the community and its longevity, a job in the community and its longevity, and anything else that might render her as one who would not be expected to flee. The idea behind a release on O.R. is that due to personal circumstances the arrested person is particularly likely to appear in court.

Many courts have risk assessment arms which investigate O.R. applicants. Sometimes a person is granted O.R. with conditions imposed such as the wearing of a global positioning system (GPS) ankle monitor, attendance at programs, drug treatment, stay-away orders, and warrantless searches.

Sometimes after an arrest the District Attorney will choose not to prosecute the case, *i.e.*, the person arrested will not have a Complaint filed against her, and instead her bail will be refunded. Again, if she has paid a fee to a bail bondsman, then she will not be able to get that money back.

Accusation

There are several ways a criminal case can begin.

An infraction begins with the issuance of a written citation by a local law enforcement office or the District Attorney. The citation must be delivered to the person accused of committing a crime, it must say on it what crime its recipient is accused of committing, and it must require her to appear in court at a specific time for the initial hearing of the case. Many people are familiar with this process from receiving a citation for a Vehicle Code violation.

Both misdemeanor and felony cases often begin with either a citation or an arrest. Again, a citation will say on it where and when to appear. If there has been an arrest, and the arrested person is released from custody through bail or O.R., the release is frequently accompanied by a notice to appear in court at a specific time.

For some misdemeanor criminal cases the District Attorney must file a Complaint with the court. For others, the citation serves as the Complaint. The Complaint must allege facts which if proved would result in a misdemeanor conviction of the person who is accused of performing the acts alleged.

For a felony criminal case either 1) the District Attorney must file a Complaint alleging a felony, or 2) there must be a Grand Jury investigation followed by a Grand Jury Indictment (a type of crime-charging document) alleging a felony. A Grand Jury investigation is led by the District Attorney who can then present the results of the investigation to a Grand Jury, which is a panel of persons appointed by the court to review information and determine if chargeable criminal activity has occurred.

Procedural Steps Before Trial

The first step after a misdemeanor or felony case has begun is the holding of a court hearing called an Arraignment. At the Arraignment, the accused (the person against whom a Complaint has been filed or an Indictment issued) is formally told of the charges, and of some of her rights, and if she is at that point in time incarcerated, she will almost certainly be given the right to post bail or be released on her own recognizance. She will enter a plea to the charges (see below).

If the District Attorney files a Complaint alleging a felony, the accused is entitled to have what is called a Preliminary Hearing. That hearing takes place before a judge without a jury, and the District Attorney has the burden to prove to the judge the probability of the accused having committed the felony. If the District Attorney meets its burden, *i.e.*, is successful in proving that probability, then the accused is "bound over" for trial, and the District Attorney must file a new form of crime-charging document, similar to the Complaint, called an Information. An Arraignment will follow from that.

If there is a Grand Jury Indictment, then there will be no Preliminary Hearing, and instead the accused goes to trial without the need for any other filing, although an Arraignment will follow.

A process known as Discovery takes place where the District Attorney must disclose to the accused's attorney the evidence that exists showing guilt of the accused, or as she is formally referred to at that point, the "defendant." The District Attorney is also required to disclose to the defendant any exculpatory evidence which the District Attorney is aware of.

Motions can be filed by either side asking for orders from the court affecting the case. For example, if the defendant's attorney believes evidence was acquired illegally, then a motion to exclude that evidence from use at trial may be made. A motion consists of the District Attorney or the defendant's attorney formally applying to the court for an order.

Trials are required to take place within a relatively short period of time after an Arraignment. For felonies, trial must begin within 60 days of the Arraignment on an Information or Indictment. For misdemeanors, if the defendant is in custody then trial must begin within 30 days of Arraignment; if the defendant is not in custody it is 45 days. If trial does not begin within its required time period, then the court is required to dismiss the charges against the defendant. Defendants can "waive time," *i.e.*, the requirement that trial occur within so many days. If the defendant is in custody, it may not be to her advantage to waive time. But if free on bail or on O.R., defendants usually will waive the requirement of trial within a specific period of time, due to the consequence of not doing so – if the case is dismissed due to the trial not occurring within the required time, the District Attorney will usually be able to file new charges, requiring a new arrest, Arraignment, *etc.*, things a defendant would want to avoid.

Private Attorney vs. Public Defender

One charged with an infraction has the right to be represented by an attorney, but she does not have a right to have an attorney appointed for her if she is financially unable to hire an attorney herself. One charged with a misdemeanor or felony does have a right to appointment of an attorney free of charge if she is financially destitute. It is common for counties to have a Public Defender's office which is financed by the state and which represents indigent criminal defendants. Counties without a Public Defender's office pay private attorneys to do this work on a case by case basis. The ability of the family of a criminal defendant to hire an attorney has no bearing on the right of an indigent defendant to appointment of an attorney free of charge. If a defendant lacks the financial ability, and her family is able, the family might want to hire a private attorney. This is a matter of one's individual choice, and those making the choice should bear in mind several things: 1) The Public Defenders and private attorneys appointed by courts to represent indigent defendants are experts in criminal law and procedure, and almost surely have experience in dealing with persons with mental illnesses. 2) Private attorneys can be expensive to hire. 3) If before trial a Public Defender or appointed private attorney should appear to be deficient in some way in representing a defendant, she could then be replaced by a retained private attorney when there is money to pay the private attorney and if the defendant agrees to this. 4) If a defendant is repeatedly arrested and repeatedly demands that her family come to her aid by hiring a private attorney, it might be beneficial to her to have her demands denied, and to know that she will need to face all consequences that befall one who is charged with committing a crime. 5) One who suffers from a mental illness may not be able to understand she has committed a crime or may be unable to form the specific intent needed to commit some crimes, and the attorney – public or private – must be aware of the nature of the mental illness suffered by the defendant and be able to present it as a defense. (See H. below.)

Criminal cases are complicated, and they sometimes require a criminal law specialist to handle the case on behalf of the defendant. A defendant should never represent herself.

Diversion from the Criminal Justice System

Under certain circumstances a criminal case will qualify for "diversion." This means that due to policy considerations it is allowable for a court to handle a charged offense not by trial and then punishment if a conviction, but instead for the charged offense to be disposed of without a contest over guilt or innocence and without a penalty of fine or incarceration. What happens is that the defendant is allowed to obtain counseling and/or attend an educational program, and upon completion the criminal charges are dismissed against her. Some counties have special mental health courts to handle these types of cases when the defendant has a mental illness, and they will often require compliance with a treatment plan for some substantial period of time before charges are dismissed. A defendant's attorney, public or private, is able to determine if the defendant is eligible for diversion and can present an application to the court for diversion and propose a plan.

Competency to Stand Trial

The District Attorney, the defendant's attorney, and/or the court are able to raise the issue of whether one is mentally competent to stand trial, although this is usually done by the defendant's attorney. The test of a defendant's mental competence is whether she is able to understand the nature and purpose of the criminal proceedings against her to the extent that she can assist in her defense.

A defendant's attorney raises the issue of competency formally or informally with the judge and District Attorney. If the District Attorney agrees to what is called a "preliminary evaluation" (which varies from court to court but essentially includes a mental health expert's review and report), then a preliminary evaluation, consisting of a somewhat informal evaluation, can be ordered by the judge. Either before or after the preliminary evaluation, if a judge has a reasonable doubt as to whether the defendant is competent, and that doubt is based on substantial evidence, then the judge must initiate mental competency proceedings.

Once the issue of competency is initiated, the criminal proceedings are suspended, and the court appoints at least one qualified psychologist or psychiatrist to evaluate the defendant and to submit a written report offering an opinion on whether the defendant is currently competent to stand trial. Both the District Attorney and the defendant's attorney will have the opportunity to review the report and advise the court as to whether they agree with the findings and opinion offered. If both sides do not agree on this, then a trial on the issue will take place, either solely before the judge or with a jury, at the defendant's option. At a trial the defendant's attorney can present additional evidence, *i.e.*, the defendant can call its own experts and other witnesses. If the defendant is found competent to stand trial, then criminal proceedings will be reinstated immediately, and the case continues from the point where it was pending when suspended.

If the defendant is found incompetent to stand trial, then the court will order a commitment to a state hospital or other treatment facility until she becomes competent. If the defendant has not gained competence to stand trial within a maximum of three years after commitment, the court must refer the case to the county to institute a type of LPS Conservatorship for her. To distinguish this type of conservatorship from the one described in Chapter 2, this kind is generally referred to as a Murphy Conservatorship.[24]

Pre-Trial Disposition, Trial, and Appeal

The plea the defendant enters at the Arraignment can be either guilty, not guilty, or no contest.

If the plea is guilty, then the judge will find her guilty of the crime. The District Attorney and the defendant and her attorney will then have the right to be heard on the issue of punishment type, and a punishment will be prescribed by the court. Before sentencing the court

---

[24] This is named after the California State legislator who authored and promoted the law enabling this process.

often directs its Probation Department to investigate the defendant and recommend punishment (see section L. below).

If the plea is not guilty, then the case must be tried. If the crime charged is an infraction, then the trial will take place before a judge without a jury. If the crime is a misdemeanor or felony, then the trial will be before a judge or a jury, at the option of the defendant. A judge will supervise the jury trial, and if there is a conviction it is the judge who will determine the punishment. An exception to this is where the punishment sought by the District Attorney is death, in which case the jury will hear evidence on that issue and make that decision.

The effect in the criminal case of a no contest plea is the same as that of a guilty plea. The difference between them relates to a claim in a civil case for damages, as a no contest plea cannot be used against the person entering it as evidence of her civil liability whereas a guilty plea can be.

Before the date set for trial, a Pre-Trial Conference will be set where the defendant and her attorney will meet with a judge and the District Attorney. The defendant and the District Attorney can reach an agreement that the defendant will change her plea of not guilty to guilty or to no contest to the crime charged, or to a different crime, in exchange for dismissal of other charges or a recommendation of a more lenient sentence. This is called a plea bargain, and because of the sheer number of criminal cases relative to the number of courts available to try them, most criminal cases are resolved this way.

Unless a conviction is agreed to by the defendant and the District Attorney, conviction of a crime can only occur after a trial where the trier of fact – either judge or jury – finds there is no reasonable doubt that the defendant committed the crime charged.[25] For a jury to convict, every juror must agree there is an absence of a reasonable doubt that the defendant committed the crime charged. If there is a trial to a judge

---

[25] This standard of proof is known as "beyond a reasonable doubt."

without a jury, and the judge has a reasonable doubt, or if there is a jury trial and all jurors have a reasonable doubt, then a finding of not guilty must be entered. A finding of not guilty means the case is over, and the defendant is forever free of the charge. A not guilty finding is not a finding of innocence, as innocence is not something a defendant must prove or need to establish in any way. To the contrary, it is the District Attorney who has the burden of proof to establish guilt. As said, if the judge as the trier of fact cannot determine that the defendant is guilty beyond a reasonable doubt, then the defendant must be found not guilty. If one or more, but less than all jurors, have a reasonable doubt, then the jury is said to be deadlocked, or "hung." The hung jury arises when not all jurors can find guilt beyond a reasonable doubt (which would require a finding of guilty), yet not all jurors have a reasonable doubt (which would require a finding of not guilty). When the jury is hung, the case must either be re-tried or dismissed, at the option of the District Attorney.

If there is a conviction after a trial, the defendant has a right to appeal her conviction to another court, called an appellate court. Appeals are almost always heard only on issues of law, not issues of fact. Typical issues of law are whether the correct laws were applied by the trial judge, and whether irregularities were committed at trial which denied the defendant a fair trial. The only issue of fact that could be the subject of appeal is whether the evidence supporting the conviction cannot be interpreted in any manner so as to lead to a finding by a reasonable person that the defendant committed the charged crime.

Appellate attorneys will be appointed at the State's cost to represent indigent criminal appellants.

Sometimes an appeal can result in a finding of not guilty. However, when trial court error is found by an appellate court which is deemed by the appellate court sufficient to overturn the finding of guilty, it is most likely that the case will be sent back to the trial court for retrial or dismissal, not that the appellate court would issue a finding of not guilty.

When appeals are lost, the cases are generally over, except that a defendant who raises an issue that there was a violation of the United States Constitution can petition a Federal court for relief.

Diminished Capacity and Insanity

If due to mental illness a criminal defendant is unable to form the intent, premeditation, deliberation, or malice required of certain crimes, she cannot be found guilty of the crime. This is generally known as the defense of "diminished capacity" or "diminished responsibility." Due to its unpopularity with the electorate, it was voted out of existence in California, but the Legislature put it back in the law in a limited way, applicable only for crimes that require a "specific" intent.

Some crimes are said to require a specific intent to commit, while others need only a general intent. For example, the crime of theft requires not only taking something belonging to another, but the specific intent to deprive the owner of it permanently. The crime of assault, on the other hand, requires only an intent to attack someone, but not an intent to specifically harm the person attacked. The distinctions in this field are often fine and subtle ones, and there is a large body of law interpreting various factual situations giving rise to specific versus general intent crimes. But if one is charged with a specific intent crime, and she can establish to the trier of fact – either judge or jury – that due to her mental illness she was unable to have formed the requisite specific intent at the time of the crime, then she will be acquitted, *i.e.*, found not guilty.

If due to mental illness one is unable to form a required mental state, then she also would be eligible for a finding of not guilty by reason of insanity. One is not guilty of a crime if she can establish that as a result of her mental illness she was insane to the extent of being incapable of understanding the nature and quality of her alleged criminal act and was incapable of distinguishing right from wrong at the time of the act. This is a mental state that goes beyond that of diminished capacity, but again the distinctions can be fine and subtle, and again, there is a large body of law which has interpreted the rules and how they apply to various factual situations. If a defendant raises this defense, she is first tried on the guilt or innocence of the crime without reference to this defense, and then if she is found guilty, the issue of insanity at the time of the criminal act is tried, and if it is established that she was insane at the time, then she will be acquitted of the crime. If acquitted, she will be committed to a state hospital until she gains sanity at which point she will be released, unless the court finds that she has already regained sanity, in which case she will be immediately released.

If a criminal defendant fails at her attempt to prove either diminished capacity to form a specific intent, or insanity, then at sentencing she still is entitled to raise her diminished capacity as an ameliorating factor in the crime. Thus, the defendant actually has a second chance to show diminished capacity due to mental illness. If established, it will not at this point lead to an acquittal, but it can lead to a reduced punishment.

Establishing a disabling mental illness can be complicated and difficult. While it can be done with psychiatric testimony and opinion, the District Attorney has the opportunity to refute this testimony with psychiatric testimony presenting a contrary opinion. Typically, the more egregious the crime, the greater the resistance to a mental illness defense that can be expected from the District Attorney. But this is not always the situation, as there are some cases where a disabling mental illness is so obvious that a District Attorney will not even challenge a claimed mental illness defense, and the case will not need to be tried.

Jail Visits

Each jail has its own rules, but usually each jail has visiting days and hours it establishes for anyone wanting to visit an inmate, and a reservation is required. An inmate's attorney is not limited to the normal visiting times and can visit the inmate at all reasonable times. Telephone visits are often possible, but again each jail typically has its own rules that must be learned and followed.

It is important to keep in mind that all jail calls are recorded, and since conversations therefore are not confidential, they are allowed to be used as evidence by the District Attorney against the defendant.

Punishment

Penalties imposed after a conviction of committing a crime run the gamut from community service to a fine to restitution to victims (see section O. below) to probation to a suspended sentence to commitment to county jail to commitment to state prison to death. There are sentencing guidelines, and within those guidelines each case necessarily stands on its own. Typically, after a felony conviction occurs the judge will refer the matter to the county Probation Department for investigation and report to the court on the defendant's situation and a recommended sentence.

Often the punishments are combined. For example, it is common for a criminal defendant who is convicted of a misdemeanor or felony which is nonviolent in nature, and who is not a repeat offender, to be given a sentence consisting of probation and community service.

Probation means that for a specified period of time a convicted defendant (an "offender") is subject to court supervision. An offender may be assigned a Probation Officer from the county Probation Department who monitors her behavior and any conditions of her probation. In the vast majority of cases no Probation Officer is assigned, and it is then solely up to the court to monitor the probation conditions. A common condition is that the offender perform a specified number of hours of community service. The offender will be given a list of organizations with which she can perform these services. If she does not complete the performance within a specified period of time, then her probation will be revoked, and she will spend the remainder of her probation period in a county jail or state prison. One accused of a probation violation is entitled to a hearing on the issue, but there is no right to a jury, and the standard of proof is what is called a preponderance of the evidence, which means the judge at that hearing concludes it is more likely than not that the violation did or did not occur.

A suspended sentence works much as probation does. An offender is given a jail or prison sentence, and then it is suspended (not carried out) with conditions attached. If a violation of the conditions of the sentence occurs, the sentence will become unsuspended. Mandatory mental health treatment can be made a condition for a suspended sentence or probation.

The District Attorney and the defendant will likely recommend penalties different from each other. Again, the decision is for the judge to make, except in capital cases where the jury will decide.

If jail or prison time is given, then the defendant will have a right to be released after serving between 50% - 80% of the sentence (depending on the crime) if she has not caused problems while incarcerated. This is known as "good-time credit." When a defendant is released prior to completion of her full sentence, she will be placed on parole until the date the completion would have occurred. On parole she will be required to meet various conditions and restrictions, and will be supervised by a state parole officer. If she violates a condition or restriction, even if the violation is not a crime itself, she can be taken back into custody to serve out the balance of her prison term.

If a sentence of state prison is given to an offender, she will be sent to a prison that exists for her type of crime and criminal history, and for her gender, as all state prisons are segregated by gender.

Treatment of Mental Illness While Incarcerated

It is a tragic reality that a substantial percentage of persons in jails and prisons suffer from serious mental illnesses. While punishment for crimes may deter the commission of more crimes, it is inexplicably cruel to impose penalties on people who violate the law due to delusional thoughts or to hallucinations, or simply an inability to understand that they are engaging in illegal and unacceptable activities that hurt others. Psychiatric institutions are built and operated according to a therapeutic model; prisons are not, and their harshness could never be deemed therapeutic. Yet the fact remains that far more mentally ill persons are inmates of prisons than they are of psychiatric institutions, despite the ability of courts to find defendants to have been unable to form the mental capacity required to commit the crime charged (see section J. above).

Jails and prisons have medical providers on staff. Not all of these providers are psychiatrists or psychologists, but due to the sheer magnitude of inmates with mental illness, these providers do have some knowledge and experience in the field of mental illness. They also have an ability to provide medications to inmates with mental illness. (See below.)

If an inmate's mental health status is not already known, it likely will be discovered soon after arrival at the institution. Screenings for suicidal and other self-damaging tendencies, and for evidence of psychosis, are done at the time of admission. It is often necessary for Supporters to inform those operating the institution of a Consumer's mental health state and diagnosis, and identify the medications that she is receiving. If this is done by phone or in person, it should be followed by a letter confirming it. The Consumer's attorney can help with this.

While incarceration can interfere with a Consumer's medication intake, it can also result in a Consumer being placed on a regular medication regimen. A prisoner can be provided psychotropic medication on a scheduled basis. If she objects to it, she can be encouraged to take it, but she cannot be forced to take any medication without a court order, absent an emergency.[26]

Such a court order would be based on a Consumer's lack of capacity to refuse medication, and only would be issued after a hearing. For a Consumer in a county jail the hearing would be before a Superior Court judge, commissioner, or appointed hearing officer. For a Consumer in a state prison the hearing would be before an administrative law judge (an attorney hired by the Department of Corrections – the state department that operates its prisons – for the purpose of conducting hearings involving prisoners). For both county jail and state prison the Consumer would be entitled to appointment of an attorney to represent her at the hearing, and any Order would be valid for up to one year and would be renewable after another hearing.

An emergency allowing the involuntary administration of medication would only exist if the medication were necessary to preserve someone's life or prevent serious bodily harm. If the emergency lasts more than 72 hours then an order would be needed, and there is a procedure to obtain a temporary order pending the full hearing required.

---

[26] A Consumer's rights and the procedure to obtain a court order are spelled out in Penal Code sections 2602 and 2603.

Residual Effects of a Conviction

The legal effects of a criminal conviction include the following:

1) One convicted of a felony loses her right to vote.

2) Repeated convictions may lead to minimum sentencing of 25 years or more (commonly known as 3 strikes and you're out).

3) Criminal convictions of undocumented foreigners are ordinarily referred to the Department of Homeland Security and likely will result in deportation proceedings.

4) Depending on the crime, convicted perpetrators might be restricted from residing in certain areas or from holding certain jobs or from obtaining certain privileges such as a license to own firearms. There may also be county registration requirements.

5) Public benefits such as SSI are usually suspended when one is incarcerated for at least 30 days.

Rights of Victims and Witnesses

Specific legal rights of crime victims and crime witnesses in the criminal justice system have been delineated by the legislature.[27] Included are the right to be notified of hearings and postponements, of criminal investigation results, of case dispositions, of a pending parole or other release of a crime perpetrator, of the right to restitution from the crime perpetrator[28] and from a state fund established for crime victims, and the right to be heard at sentencing hearings. Much information on these rights is available from the Victims of Crime Resource Center of the Pacific McGeorge School of Law – www.1800victims.org – from the

---

27 Penal Code sections 679 *et seq* and 1191 *et seq*
28 Restitution directly from the crime perpetrator can be ordered by the court as part of the Judgment. See Penal Code section 1191.2.

California Victims Compensation Board – www.victims.ca.gov – and from the Victims' Services Unit of the California Attorney General – www.oag.ca.gov/victimservices.

The Legislature has declared that victims' and witnesses' rights are to be "honored and protected by law enforcement agencies, prosecutors, and judges in a manner no less vigorous than the protections afforded criminal defendants."[29]

Juveniles

Persons under the age of 18 do not go through the court system described above, and instead are subject to a completely separate system. Many procedures are the same or similar as for adults. Prominent differences for juveniles are no bail or O.R., no jury, no state hospital commitments, reduced sentencing, and no death penalty.

Conclusion

Trial and punishment of a Consumer can be a particularly severe experience for the Consumer, and for her Supporters too.

A Consumer can raise issues relating to diversion from the criminal court system, competency to stand trial, and an inability to actually commit a crime due to diminished capacity or insanity. These claims are not always appropriate or winnable ones and are often opposed by the District Attorney.

Criminal prosecution and conviction can at times have a silver lining, where a Consumer who will not cooperate with a treatment plan or even the need for treatment is put in a position where treatment is mandated. And if treatment is a failure, it is possible a Consumer will

---

[29] Penal Code section 679

learn that certain behaviors will not be tolerated and as a consequence she might modify those behaviors. Much depends on how much a Consumer can comprehend, and can control her behavior, given the nature and extent of her illness.

For a Consumer and her Supporters to suffer through the indignities of a criminal prosecution and punishment for an act which she wasn't and still might not be able to fully comprehend, can be a special form of torment and tragedy. Hopefully someday this will change, and people who are sick will not be treated like people who are willing to hurt others to gain an advantage for themselves, but like people who are sick.

CHAPTER 4

RESTRAINING ORDERS

Introduction

When a Consumer suffers from a serious mental illness which is not being treated or is not responding to treatment, her condition might deteriorate to the point where she becomes a threat to other people. If the threatening behavior is reported to authorities, and the police or other government officials investigate it and determine there is a danger sufficient to necessitate an involuntary psychiatric hold, and the hold is made, then the immediate danger will be removed, at least temporarily. (See Chapter 2.)

If there is an involuntary hold for threatening behavior, at some point the county imposing the hold will likely determine the danger necessitating the hold no longer exists, and the Consumer will be released. At that point a court order might be needed directing the Consumer to stay away from the threatened person. And if firearms are an issue, the order would need to direct her to relinquish possession of all of them to the police.

If the authorities determine that the degree of the threat does not rise to the level that would result in an involuntary hold, then the same court order might be needed protecting the threatened person.

The court orders referred to in this chapter are alternately referred to as "restraining orders" or "protective orders." They are being called restraining orders here. All restraining orders to prohibit threats of violence or harassment contain orders prohibiting contact with the threatened person and requiring the Consumer to stay away from the threatened person, and all of them also prohibit possession of a gun by the restrained person.

Events Leading to a Restraining Order

Mental illness is not predictable. Consumers who are not treated are at risk of becoming disruptive, volatile and dangerous. Even when treated, one who suffers from mental illness can remain unstable, and can experience uncontrollable symptoms. There are Consumers who respond well to treatment and who are able to keep their symptoms under control for long periods of time, yet will at some point regress, and display previous symptoms. There might be some event which triggers regression, although Supporters well know that regression can occur without anything obvious causing it. Delusions such as perceiving innocent persons as enemy conspirators, or auditory hallucinations which command one to physically weaken or remove another as a foe, are not uncommon symptoms of some types of untreated mental illness, or of treated mental illness which relapses. For anyone suffering from a severe mental illness, acts of violence resulting in physical harm are a possibility.

Many persons who regularly interact with Consumers do not immediately react to what others might see as a threatening situation. Supporters who know the individual and her usual symptoms may recognize loud or threatening words as only temporary, requiring nothing more than perhaps patience and quiet and a display of firmness and understanding, and a little passage of time. Likely a Supporter doesn't want to call the police every time her child shouts out something like, "Keep that up, and I'll kill you." Words like this can be hurtful and scary, but if they are followed not by any physical action but by a return to a relative calmness, and maybe with an apology or an acknowledgment of irrationality, and if these words do not have a history of having ever been acted upon, then a Supporter might tend to see them as a transitory expression of feelings of desperation and let them go. Like non-Consumers, Consumers sometimes says things out of frustration which they don't mean and won't act on.

Angry words are often used only as a means to release tension, and they don't necessitate a restraining order. Other times they are a warning of actions to come. It is each individual Supporter's decision as to what to leave alone and what to get help for, but there are situations we should never let slide. When a threat of immediate harm is perceived, something must be done immediately, whether the Consumer has a weapon or not. Find a safe place and call 911. When one is irrational *and* has a weapon in her possession that she appears ready to use – maybe a kitchen knife or a razor blade or a screwdriver or a hammer or a baseball bat or a pole or a stick or a gun or a rock or – then it is time to get to a safe place and call 911. When a physical assault takes place, against one's person or property, it is time to call 911. When a verbal threat is made and there is an ability to carry it through, and there is a history of violence, and the threat is not revoked soon after it is made, it is time to call 911.

Supporters may tend to hesitate to call 911 because of negative consequences of police involvement. We do not want to lose the trust of our loved ones. We don't want to cause more problems and make matters worse. However, whether or not there might be more problems created for a Consumer or a Supporter is absolutely not pertinent during a period of time when someone is at risk of physical harm. If there might be something more than a threat made solely for its effect, then help must be obtained, immediately.

If a Supporter is going to make a mistake, then the error should be on the side of caution, not on the side of injury or death. If the threat turns out to have been transitory only, nothing bad will result from calling 911. In fact, there are potential good results, as it is a strong message to a Consumer that there are boundaries she may not cross without consequences, and a very strong incentive for her not to cross those boundaries in the future. And if she is too irrational to even understand a boundary or the consequences of violating it, then her threatening words or gestures are likely a very real and serious threat, and immediate help is needed and must be obtained.

Supporters should never be afraid to call 911. If it is deemed an emergency by the person handling the call then there will be an immediate response by the police, *etc.* If not deemed an emergency, the response might not be immediate. It is not for a Supporter, under a threat of harm, to decide if it is really an emergency. Make it simple: if we think it *might be* an emergency, then we immediately call 911.

A 911 call does not mean a threat is removed. There are various scenarios that can ensue from a 911 call, and virtually all of them carry the possibility of the threat remaining unimpeded and continuing. When a threat is unabated, *i.e.*, when it continues even after a visit by the police, then a restraining order will be needed.

It is not only violence or a threat of it which will give rise to the need for a restraining order. Conduct which alarms, annoys, or harasses someone and serves no legitimate purpose is subject to being restrained by court order. The only qualifier is that the conduct must be of a type that would cause substantial emotional distress in a reasonable person.

There is an important type of restraining order that will issue without establishing harassment. It is an order issued solely to prohibit one from possessing a gun. This type of order will be issued by a court if it can be shown that there is a danger of harm, and that there is some history of gun violence or the threat of gun violence. This type of order can only by obtained by an immediate family member[30] or a law enforcement officer. Persons with delusions and hallucinations should not have guns.

Actions Preparatory to Obtaining a Restraining Order

The restraining order process requires time and energy and likely money too, so if the process can be avoided, it should be. If the police will talk to the threatening person and let her know that she is risking arrest with her behavior, that can sometimes take care of the problem. A letter from an attorney explaining future consequences also might resolve it. If neither of these will work, then a restraining order needs to be applied for.

Before applying for a restraining order, a Supporter will want to be sure that she has the evidence needed to present to the court which will be hearing the application. If there are verbal threats, a person who has heard these threats will likely need to be present in court to testify to them. Just as good would be a recording of the threats, if the recording is done legally and if the person who does the recording – and this can be the threatened person – is in court to testify to the fact of the recording and how it was carried out. Generally, recording someone's words is only legal if she has no reasonable expectation of privacy when she is speaking, such as speaking loudly in a public place, or if she knows she is being recorded. Recording someone's words is also legal if she is threatening a violent felony. It is not necessary for one recording threats to determine if the violent acts threatened are felonies or some other form of crime (see Chapter 3 for definitions of categories of crime); it is reasonable to conclude that all violent criminal acts are felonies. It also might be necessary to have a treating mental health

---

[30] An immediate family member has been defined as spouse, domestic partner, (step)parent, (step)child, (step)grandparent, (step)grandchild, (step)sibling, or anyone else who within the past 6 months resided in the household of the person being restrained. See Penal Code section 422.4(b)(3).

professional in court. Precisely what is needed depends on the precise situation. If the potential to file an application for a restraining order exists, then the applicant likely should consult with an attorney, regardless of whether or not an attorney is going to be hired to appear in court with the applicant.

The Restraining Order Application Process

Courts have simplified the restraining order procedure so that unlike most other legal proceedings it can be done without an attorney, and it is therefore not necessary to have an attorney appear in court with the applicant. Courts have established self-help centers at the courthouses to assist applicants in filling out the correct papers and using this resource might make it possible to dispense with consulting an attorney altogether.[31] The advice of an attorney can be invaluable, but there is usually a cost that accompanies it, and that can be a factor. Each situation, of course, will be different.

The exact procedures employed to obtain a restraining order depend on the county where the application is made. In all California counties the procedure basically consists of the preparation of a petition on a court-supplied form, followed by filing it with the court, service of it on the person to be restrained by someone who is not a party to the case, and a hearing. Applications are categorized as to type, *e.g.*, domestic violence, or elder abuse, or general civil harassment. The type applied for can be an important factor, depending on the facts of the case, but this is not something an applicant must know on her own. Again, it is best if an applicant can be assisted by an attorney or by someone at a court-operated self-help center, one who would know into what category the restraining order falls.

---

[31] Information on the California Courts Self-Help Center is found at www.courtinfo.ca.gov/selfhelp.

After service of the petition on the party against whom the restraining order is sought, a hearing will be held. Each side is entitled to be represented by an attorney. If there is a question as to whether an attorney will be needed, then one should be consulted.

Typically, what is called a temporary restraining order will be issued by a court before the service of the petition and the actual hearing taking place. To obtain this temporary order, an applicant must file her petition for a restraining order with the court, but before serving it she will submit it to a judicial department of the court (usually the same day it is filed, in the same building) along with a declaration that shows proof of harassment and that great or irreparable injury will be suffered by the applicant if a temporary order is not issued. The temporary order will then remain in effect only until the hearing, unless extended at that time by the court.

The actual wording of a restraining order will be dependent on the facts of the case. Usually the order will require one to stay a specified distance away from another and her home and workplace, and to refrain from contacting the protected person directly or by phone, mail, or email. All restraining orders prohibit the person whose conduct is restrained from possessing a firearm.

Sometimes a person responding to an application for a restraining order will ask for her own restraining order against the applicant. If she has filed a petition and her application is properly before the court, the court might issue restraining orders which are reciprocal. This means the original applicant would be restrained also, and this can happen even when the only evidence of a need for a restraining order against the applicant is testimony of the other party who is, at least to some degree, irrational. Sometimes it seems the reason for this being done is that it tends to simplify the process and helps to avoid conflict and stigma. However, in a situation where a mutual restraining order would in any way interfere with something of significance, such as the applicant's ability to contact and provide information to the restrained person's medical providers, or it would evidently lead to even more harassment of the applicant, then it will not be made. All pertinent factors will be considered by the court.

There is also what is called a criminal restraining order. It is an order issued by a court against one charged or convicted of a crime which restrains her from contacting the crime's victim. It can be sought by the Office of the District of Attorney which is prosecuting the crime and can be suggested and urged by the victim. (See Chapter 3.)

The Effect of a Restraining Order

There are both legal and practical effects of a restraining order. Legally, these orders work when they deter the person restrained from engaging in the bad behavior, or in the arrest of the person restrained if she disobeys the order. Practically, restraining orders tend to work because disobedience of a restraining order is a crime, and a person restrained does not want to be arrested and charged if she disobeys the order. Of course, many who commit crimes feel impervious to detection, and there are those restrained who believe they can continue their previous course of conduct because to them the order itself means nothing. One should not feel free of danger simply because a restraining order has been issued.

With respect to the type of restraining order which solely prohibits possession of a gun, if the restrained person fails to relinquish all guns, the police are authorized to obtain a search warrant in order to discover and remove any guns still in her possession.

One whose conduct is restrained by a court order might try to cajole the protected person into having the order removed. There might be an emotional plea made that the existence of the order is unfair or stigmatizing or just interferes with a family or friend relationship. There is no one answer to the question of whether an order should be voluntarily removed, as each situation is different and complicated in its own way. Perhaps a good rule of thumb is that if one protected by such an order is not 100% sure of her safety, then the order should remain in effect so it can be used if needed.

Under California law a restraining order can be made to last for up to 1, 3, or 5 years, depending on the type. For example, the duration of an order issued solely to prohibit possession of a gun is limited to 1 year; an order issued to prevent workplace violence is limited to 3 years; and an order issued to prevent harassment is limited to 5 years. All restraining orders can be renewed with a new application within 3 months of their expiration dates.

Significantly, there are various laws which require law enforcement agencies to enforce restraining orders, and to cooperate with each other in the enforcement process.

Conclusion

The decision whether to obtain a restraining order is dependent on a number of factors, and it must be made on an individual basis, situation by situation. Sometimes a restraining order is absolutely necessary to avoid existing or potential harm. Other times it might be deemed excessive considering the lack of a credible threat, and could cause additional conflict, although these times would be relatively rare. Again, it is always better to err on the side of caution, and if it is believed that a threat might exist, and there is no other way to prevent it, then a restraining order should be applied for.

Safety first is a good motto. The restraining order procedure has been streamlined and made as simple as possible, and with the enforcement of restraining orders mandated by law, the procedure has real teeth. Restraining orders should be employed as needed.

CHAPTER 5

GOVERNMENT PROGRAMS AND BENEFITS

Introduction

Numerous federal, state, and local government programs exist to aid those with severe mental illnesses. These programs contain what is commonly referred to as *public* benefits. The rules of these programs are frequently complicated and confusing. The purpose of this chapter is to make reference to the programs most commonly accessed by Consumers and to try to put their more important provisions in relatively easy to understand terms.

Social Security Supplemental Security Income (SSI)

SSI is a federal program operated by the Social Security Administration (the SSA).[32] It provides a monthly cash stipend to qualified persons. Recipients must qualify both medically and financially. The amount of the monthly payment, which is dependent on factors such as locale and other sources of income, is relatively small, yet for a person with a serious mental illness the money provided is usually crucial, frequently the difference between having a home and being homeless. In order to

---

[32] 42 United States Code (hereinafter *USC*) sections 1381 *et seq*

govern the operation of the program, the SSA is empowered to and has established Regulations.[33] The Regulations essentially have the effect of laws that are enacted by Congress.

Qualification and Maintaining Benefits

To qualify for, or to stay qualified for SSI, an applicant or recipient must meet the following tests:

1) Have a diagnosed illness which prevents her from full time, compensated work;

2) Have limited monthly cash receipts; and

3) Have no more than $2,000.00 worth of certain liquid assets.

The application process requires that a medical professional provide a report showing a diagnosis, along with an opinion based on the diagnosis that the applicant is too ill to work full time for compensation. The process also requires that the applicant not have a right to receive cash from another which could provide for all of her food and housing, and that the applicant not have "countable resources" of more than $2,000.00. The financial rules for qualifying and for staying qualified are complex; following are the basic ones:

An applicant/recipient of SSI can work and earn up to $65.00/month (called "earned income") without that compensation affecting her right to receive SSI, and without it affecting the amount of SSI she will receive. If she has earned income of more than $65.00/month then the excess would reduce her monthly SSI payment by $1.00 for every $2.00 earned, up to the point where the reduction would result in no benefits, and thus a failure to qualify for SSI, or a termination of it.

If an applicant/recipient receives more than $20.00 in cash in any one month for something other than compensation for work (called

---

[33] 20 Code of Federal Regulations (hereinafter *CFR*) Part 416

"unearned income") it would reduce her SSI benefits $1.00 for every $1.00 received. At some point this too would result in no benefits, and thus a failure to qualify for SSI, or a termination of it.

If an applicant/recipient is entitled to receive cash, for example as a beneficiary of a decedent's estate, then the SSA will charge her with receiving it at the point in time when it is due and payable, whether it is actually paid to her or not. So, when a Consumer has a right to receive money which would disqualify her from SSI or reduce her SSI stipend, simply instructing the payor of that money not to pay it to the Consumer would not qualify the Consumer for SSI, nor enable her to receive maximum benefits. Neither would giving the money away. Importantly though, there are ways to protect inheritances and other windfalls and still attain or retain eligibility for SSI, as set out below and as more fully explained in Chapter 7 and in Chapter 9.

SSI exists for the purpose of paying for housing and food. If the housing or food costs of a Consumer are paid by someone else (called a 3rd party) directly to the provider of housing or food, with funds other than or in addition to the SSI stipend, this would be treated differently than is earned income or unearned income received by the Consumer. The difference is that these 3rd party payments would likely reduce SSI benefits, but only in a limited amount; it would not terminate them.

The reduction for 3rd party payments for food and housing is calculated by using a method provided for by the SSA Regulations; currently the maximum reduction is approximately $280.00 per month. This means that if a Supporter (a 3rd party) subsidizes the cost of housing or food for a Consumer who is receiving or is applying for SSI, and the subsidy is made by paying the provider of the housing or food directly, then these payments will not disqualify the Consumer from SSI eligibility. The subsidy would result in a reduction in the Consumer's monthly SSI benefits, but the reduction currently would be no more than approximately $280.00.

This 3rd party subsidy for food and housing cannot be made by a cash payment to the SSI applicant/recipient; that would constitute unearned income. Instead, the payments must be made directly to the provider of housing or food. Again, if cash is paid to the SSI recipient (unearned income), she will have her monthly benefits reduced $1.00 for every $1.00 received over and above the first $20/month, up to the maximum amount she could receive as her SSI stipend, at which point she would be disqualified for SSI. So, if for example, a Consumer is receiving $900.00/month as her maximum SSI stipend, and she receives a monthly cash gift of $850.00, then after reducing her unearned income by the $20.00/month allowed her, her SSI stipend would be reduced by $830.00/month. But if the $850.00 were paid instead to the Consumer's landlord, then the reduction of monthly SSI would likely be approximately $280.00.

The SSA calls most liquid assets "countable resources," and limits them to a maximum of $2,000.00 for an SSI applicant/recipient. What this means is that if one owns countable resources worth more than $2,000.00, she is ineligible for SSI during the month she owns those excessive countable resources. Owning countable resources means that title to liquid assets which are not exempt is either in the name of the SSI applicant/recipient, or that she is entitled to have them transferred into her name. If she possesses cash, she is deemed to own the cash.

There are liquid assets which the SSA deems exempt from the countable resources limit. Examples are household items such as furniture and a television, a telephone, a computer, personal effects, and an automobile used for transportation. As all of these items are exempt, their values are not calculated for the purpose of determining a Consumer's countable resources. SSA also deems ownership of a home where the Consumer resides as exempt from the countable resources limit.

The SSI application process is not always as simple and straightforward as we would like it to be, and sometimes applicants need professional assistance. There are private claims representatives and private attorneys who are knowledgeable and experienced in this field and can help, for a fee. If the assistance is related to the application for SSI, the fee is usually paid out of the benefits received after qualifying, and this can often be a good investment.

SSI applications are frequently denied, for various reasons. Reviews and appeals by the SSA are allowed if timely presented and are often successful. If an application has been denied, it might be particularly useful to hire a claims representative or an attorney to handle the next steps.

As set out above, eligibility rules which apply to applicants for SSI continue to apply once a Consumer has qualified for SSI and is receiving it. The SSA normally mails recipients of SSI a questionnaire to fill out once a year in order to show the extent of their assets and income, and what has been done with their monthly SSI payments. The SSA also has access to bank records which will show if an SSI recipient has disqualifying assets or income in a formal account.

Sometimes an SSI recipient will receive a gift of money or property which would disqualify her from eligibility. Again, one cannot generally give away assets in order to attain or retain eligibility for SSI, but there are ways to use or protect an otherwise disqualifying gift in a way that establishes or preserves eligibility, as mentioned below and as more fully explained in Chapter 9.

Receipts of Gifts

When a Consumer receives a gift, it is deemed by the SSA to be countable income in the month it is received, and to the extent it is still owned by the Consumer in the following calendar month it is deemed to be a countable resource. Again, an SSI recipient cannot simply give away a gift received, or even refuse it, and still maintain eligibility for SSI. But she can use a gift to purchase exempt items (see below) that will not be deemed part of her countable resources and therefore would allow her to maintain her eligibility. And as explained in Chapter 9, she can, under certain circumstances, use the gift to fund a certain type of trust established for her benefit which will remove the value of the gift from her countable resources, and thus allow her to maintain eligibility.

If an SSI recipient has a windfall such that her countable resources exceed the $2,000.00 limit, she can "spend down" the money to under $2,000.00 by purchasing items which are exempt from the resources limits. Spending down so that a Consumer's countable resources are below the $2,000.00 limit can be an effective way to maintain SSI eligibility. Again, exempt resources include household items such as furniture and a television, telephone, computer, and a car for transportation, and personal effects. So, if, *e.g.*, an SSI recipient received a gift of $25,000.00 by way of inheritance, then she could use that money to purchase an automobile for transportation (assuming that purchase would be a wise use of the money), and the automobile would qualify as an exempt asset, and eligibility would continue.

Purchases of services are also a valid way of spending down assets to maintain eligibility. *E.G.*, using the money to pay for gym membership, school tuition, case management, and travel and transportation costs is an allowable way to spend down cash so that a Consumer's countable resources will be less than $2,000.00.

If a gift is too large to spend down effectively, or if it is needed for future expenses more crucial to the SSI recipient than an automobile or a vacation, then the SSI recipient would need to transfer the assets to a certain type of trust which is more fully discussed in Chapter 9.

Sometimes there are payments that are made for a Consumer on a more regular basis, or on an as-needed basis. *E.G.*, a Supporter might want to supplement SSI by paying for items a Consumer needs. These payments would seem to constitute "gifts." The payments are allowed, *i.e.*, either they are not characterized by the SSA as gifts or they are characterized as exempt gifts. But they are allowed only on condition that they have been made directly to vendors of goods and services and not made to the Consumer. Again, a Consumer can receive only $65.00/month in wages and $20.00/month in gifts without the money adversely affecting her SSI. The rules for money going directly to a provider of goods or services are treated differently than money paid to a Consumer. Most payments to providers of goods and services that do not constitute housing or food will not disrupt SSI eligibility nor the amount of the monthly stipend.

Again, if any payments are made to providers of housing or food, then they would reduce the SSI stipend, but they will only reduce it by a maximum of approximately $280.00/month. The SSA has detailed rules on what constitute housing costs – they include rent, mortgage payments, utilities, real estate taxes and insurance, and home maintenance and repairs.

Representative Payees

When an SSI recipient is unable to handle her own finances, the SSA will appoint a *representative payee* to receive the monthly benefits and use them for the SSI recipient. The payee must maintain a separate bank account for the SSI benefits and not commingle the SSI funds with any other funds. The payee must use the money for the recipient's current maintenance costs including food, shelter, clothing, medical care, and items that provide personal comfort. The payee also must promptly notify the SSA of any changes in the recipient's financial situation such as obtaining or losing a job, and receipts of gifts that would take the recipient's assets over the $2,000.00 limit. The payee also must report on any institutionalization of the recipient which lasts for more than 30 days as that would suspend payments, and on any positive change in the recipient's disabling illness which might render her employable.[34]

Serving as a payee is often an essential job, and also often an essentially thankless job. The SSI stipend must be protected, and the recipient is apt to want more money spent on her than is possible,

---

[34] 20 CFR Sections 404.2035, 404.2040, 416.635, and 416.640

causing conflicts. The SSA requires written accounting reports and will frequently call in the payee for time-consuming and what can feel like reproachful face to face meetings even after the written reports are submitted. Ongoing, detailed records must be kept, and current information on the recipient's living and medical and work situation must be maintained.

There are professionals who serve as payees for a fee, but a need for SSI indicates a reduced ability to pay for a professional payee. So, like all else Supporters do for Consumers, serving as a payee is usually done as a volunteer.

Social Security Disability Insurance (SSDI)

SSDI is a federal program administered by the SSA.[35] It is commonly referred to as "disability" and it exists mainly for disabled persons who have worked some minimum number of hours over a period of years and paid some minimal number of dollars into the Social Security system by way of Social Security taxes. As with SSI, an applicant for SSDI must be medically unable to work. But unlike SSI, there is no asset limit nor is there any unearned income limit. Currently there is a limitation on earned income of $1,260.00 per month.

There is a type of SSDI which the SSA calls "Childhood Disability Benefits" (CDB). It is available for one who became disabled before age 22, who is unmarried, and who has a parent either receiving Social Security retirement or disability benefits, or who died while receiving them.[36] This Consumer benefits from her parent's Social Security taxes, and she is not required to have worked and paid into the Social Security system herself. The entitlement is to an amount equal to 50% of the amount the Consumer's parent is entitled to receive. It does not reduce the parent's stipend. If the Consumer also qualifies for SSI

---

[35] 42 USC Sections 401(b) and 420-425
[36] 20 CFR 404.350 *et seq*

and would be entitled to a larger stipend from SSI, then she will receive an SSI payment for the difference.[37] A CDB recipient also will qualify for Medicare after two years, although depending on her financial condition she might be charged a Medicare premium. Just as with SSDI for Consumers who have paid into the Social Security system, eligibility for CDB is conditioned on any wages being below the threshold amount which, again, is $1,260.00 per month.

It is often critical to determine whether a Consumer is receiving SSI or SSDI or both, since again, SSI has an asset limitation and a cash receipt limitation that SSDI does not have. For example, one receiving SSDI who receives an inheritance will not become disqualified from SSDI regardless of how large the inheritance is. It can be difficult to determine whether a Consumer is on SSI or SSDI. When corresponding with a Consumer the SSA does not routinely identify the program involved. Like so many other things Social Security-related, it can take an inordinate amount of time and energy to find out something that could be made simpler. As a rule of thumb, the less a Consumer has worked in the past, the more likely it is that her benefits are SSI. But even so, she might be receiving CDB, having qualified through a parent.

Medicaid

Medicaid is another federal program,[38] although it is administered by each state, under the name given to it by each state. In California it is called *Medi-Cal*, and it is administered by the California Department of Health Care Services.[39] It pays for some medical and dental expenses

---

[37] If a Consumer qualifies for CDB she does not have the option of foregoing it and simply taking her SSI. The SSA requires an SSI applicant/recipient to avail herself of all other sources of income, and that includes CDB. But since she will receive the difference as SSI if the SSI payment would be larger than the CDB payment, she loses nothing by being required to take CDB.

[38] 42 USC sections 1396-1396w-5

[39] Welfare and Institutions Code sections 14000 *et seq* and 22 California Code of Regulations (hereinafter *CCR*) sections 50000 *et seq*

and is often vital for a Consumer as it pays for psychotropic medications which are frequently essential and expensive.

One qualifies automatically for Medicaid if she has qualified for SSI. If one is on SSDI instead of SSI, then she will need to apply separately for Medicaid. As with SSI, to qualify for Medicaid her countable resources must be under $2,000.00. There are also limitations on income, which are complicated and not subject to a simplified explanation other than this: if medical expenses would deplete one's income to what is deemed to be below a "maintenance need" level, then she is deemed to be "medically needy," and will qualify.[40]

Unlike SSI or SSDI, the Medicaid program contains a reimbursement right for the money it has paid out. Each state's Medicaid system has the right to seek reimbursement after a Consumer's death for benefits paid out for certain types of institutional care of a Consumer at any age, and for medical and dental care of a Consumer after age 55. Of course, a Consumer can only qualify for Medi-Cal if she owns less than $2,000.00 in most liquid assets, but her exempt assets would eventually be subject to reimbursement claims.

One situation where the state would seek reimbursement is when the Consumer owns an exempt asset such as a home used as the Consumer's residence. In this situation the state cannot and will not seek reimbursement until the home is sold, either before or after the Consumer's death.

Another situation where the State would seek reimbursement is when a Consumer acquires assets. This could occur in a number of ways, but the most likely way is by inheritance from a decedent who leaves assets outright to the Consumer. An acquisition of assets by a Medicaid recipient in excess of $2,000.00 would result in a disqualification for Medicaid and an obligation to reimburse the state for institutional care

---

[40] 42 CFR section 435.4; Welfare and Institutions Code sections 14005.7 and 14005.12; and 22 CCR section 50203

paid by Medicaid at any age and for medical and dental care paid for by Medicaid after age 55. This disqualification and reimbursement can be forestalled or even eliminated, as explained in Chapter 9.

Supporters will sometimes establish a type of trust that is known either as a "special needs trust" or "supplemental needs trust," and use their own money to fund it. A main purpose of this trust is to provide funds for a Consumer without it affecting the Consumer's right to public benefits. Supporters may be concerned that assets they have placed in a special needs trust will end up going to the state for Medicaid reimbursement, either before or after the Consumer's death. If the special needs trust is a type known as a 3rd party special needs trust, *i.e.*, a special needs trust established by a Supporter and funded with assets of the Supporter, the state has no reimbursement rights. This is because the trust assets are never owned by the Consumer/trust beneficiary, and thus are never subject to Medicaid reimbursement rights. Medicaid reimbursement rights only exist against assets owned by a Consumer. See Chapter 7 for a fuller explanation of this.

There are different types of Medicaid. For example, there is Medicaid to pay for physicians and hospitals and drugs, and there is Medicaid to pay for custodial care accompanied by medical care. Eligibility and reimbursement requirements differ in some respects by type, and eligibility might hinge on the age or the type of assets owned by an applicant. There are a great many variables, and it is not feasible to include them here.

Medicare

After two years of receiving SSDI, a Consumer will qualify for Medicare,[41] which is another federal medical assistance program. Often

---

[41] 42 USC sections 1395 *et seq*

one receiving SSDI qualifies for both Medicaid and Medicare, in which situation both programs will contribute to medical expenses.

Housing

There are many federal and local housing programs for persons with low incomes, and available to those suffering from severe mental illness, too many to list and explain here. The most comprehensive program is what is called *public housing*.

Public housing is a federal program established by Congress[42] and administered by the Department of Housing and Urban Development (HUD). HUD contracts with local government housing authorities to run the operations in each city or county in the United States. Only minimal rent is charged tenants who qualify financially. Housing is provided at a reduced rent in a housing development or project, or rent for private housing is subsidized through the program commonly known as *Section 8*.

Section 8 provides rent subsidies and home purchase assistance. HUD issues vouchers to supplement rent and other housing payments. HUD calls its Section 8 sub-program the *Housing Choice Voucher (HCV) Program*.[43]

Applications for public housing are made to the local housing authority, *i.e.*, the city or county office that administers publicly funded housing. Eligibility is based on the ratio of the income of a Consumer and her co-resident family members to the median income of that locale, so eligibility standards are different in each locale. There are no asset limitations, such as there are with SSI and Medicaid. HUD funds are severely limited, and there is a waiting list, and on the list there is criteria

---

[42] 42 USC sections 1404a-1440
[43] The Regulations established by HUD are found at 24 CFR sections 982 *et seq.*

– such as existing homelessness – for moving ahead of others on the list.

Local housing authorities are given flexibility in administering the program, and as a result the rules differ from local jurisdiction to local jurisdiction, as do the interpretations of the laws and the HUD Regulations. There are thousands of local jurisdictions in the United States, and with each making its own interpretations, income of and distributions from special needs trusts (see Chapter 7) or distributions from Supporters are sometimes inconsistently charged as income to recipients or applicants by different housing authorities. Some housing authorities do not use such earnings and distributions in calculating a Consumer's income, although most do. When a Consumer establishes a self-settled special needs trust (see Chapter 9) housing authorities will frequently penalize the Consumer for transferring assets for less than fair market value (even though this is allowed by the SSA) by imputing income from the trust to the Consumer, *i.e.*, treating income of that trust as though it has been paid directly to the Consumer.

With its HCV program, HUD contracts with an eligible applicant's landlord, and requires in its contract that the property be maintained according to certain minimum standards, and that inspections be allowed to verify this. Unless there are local prohibitions against it, landlords can often legally discriminate against HCV applicants by refusing to contract with HUD to accept HCV money. Some landlords may discriminate because they do not want poor or mentally ill people living in their buildings (which is not legal; see Chapter 12). Some may do it because they do not want to conform to the maintenance and inspection requirements of the HCV program, and again, absent local rules to the contrary or a specifically illegal purpose, a refusal to accept HCV subsidies is legal.

Many Consumers reside in group homes which exist for mental health consumers. They are frequently privately owned and operated and are regulated by local governments. Residence in a group home for disabled persons qualifies as housing that is eligible for an HCV subsidy.

In-Home Supportive Services

If a Consumer is unable to perform her own personal care services, then depending on her financial situation, she may be eligible for In-Home Supportive Services (IHSS). IHSS is a California program with federal contributions for disabled low-income persons.[44] The California Department of Social Services directs the administration of the program with involvement from the California Department of Health Care Services. Each county administers the program for its eligible residents. IHSS will pay for domestic workers, transporters, protective services, and paramedical services. Often it will pay a family member to provide the needed services for a Consumer.

A Consumer who is eligible for SSI automatically qualifies financially for IHSS. If a Consumer has higher income than is allowed by SSI she may still qualify for IHSS, but she will be required to share in the cost of the services provided.

Significantly, a Consumer must qualify for IHSS on the basis of need, *i.e.*, establish that she is unable to live completely independently, and lacks the financial ability to remedy this, and therefore needs IHSS to help her survive on her own. Accordingly, IHSS services are provided in different ways, depending on the need.

---

[44] 42 USC sections 1396 and 1397; 45 CFR pt 96; California Welfare and Institutions Code sections 10000-10002, 11000, 12300 *et seq*, 14132.95, and 15000-15001; and 22 CCR 51003.3 *et seq*.

Veterans' Benefits

The Veterans Administration (VA) runs numerous federal programs for persons who have served in the U.S. armed forces.[45]

The most commonly known VA program is for medical care, which includes psychiatric and psychological treatment, both in-patient and out-patient, and which is provided through local VA medical centers. The services are free.

There is a program that pays monthly compensation to veterans with disabilities which are the result of an injury or a disease, or aggravation of an injury or disease, that occurred during their period of military service. The amount paid is not dependent on a veteran's income or assets, but on the veteran's degree of disability and number of dependents. And if a veteran dies as a result of a service-connected disability, then her survivors will be entitled to benefits from this program.

There is a VA program that pays monthly compensation to wartime veterans who have limited assets and income, and either are totally and permanently disabled or are older than 64. The disability need not have been the result of the veteran's service.

There is a VA program that provides education and vocational rehabilitation benefits.

There are programs run by the California Department of Veterans Affairs for disabled veterans which include free tuition for disabled veterans at California colleges.

There are California property tax exemptions available for veterans.

---

[45] Title 38, CFR

All of these programs are significant given there are a large number of veterans with mental illness and with physical and psychological injuries derived from participation in wars.

Special Education

Special Education is a federally funded program[46] that provides for assisted instruction in public schools for disabled minors. It is free to a qualifying Consumer and her parents. The program is administered by individual schools which determine eligibility and set up a plan for each student in the program. Services provided vary depending on need.

Food Stamps

This is a federally funded program subsidizing food costs for financially needy persons. In California it is administered by the Department of Social Services, and bears the name, "CalFresh.[47] In order to qualify, one must have income below the federal poverty line, and her assets must be worth less than $2,000.00. There is also an exception where one with assets and income that would otherwise disqualify her can qualify if she is living with a Medi-Cal eligible person. The eligibility rules are complex and differ a bit state to state. A Consumer receiving SSI is eligible for this subsidy in all states, even though one of the stated purposes of SSI is to cover the cost of food.

Conclusion

As shown, there are numerous government programs to assist Consumers. And, there are even more programs than these most

---

[46] 7 USC Sections 2011 *et seq*
[47] Welfare and Institutions Code Sections 18900 *et seq*

common ones listed. Possibly none of them are completely adequate, but all of them do have significant value for the vast majority of Consumers.

One caveat: It is not unheard of for applicants and recipients of public benefits to fail to disclose all assets or income. An intentional failure to disclose them constitutes a serious crime, and the government will prosecute this crime. If one needs public benefits but doesn't qualify financially, there may be legal ways to deal with the situation in order to qualify. Hiding money is not one of those ways. There are things worse than not receiving public benefits. One of them is not receiving public benefits while residing in prison.

Lastly, it is not always clear whether one qualifies for particular public benefits. But usually no harm is done by applying for them.

CHAPTER 6

LIABILITY OF SUPPORTERS

Introduction

Sometimes persons suffering from a severe mental illness engage in conduct which causes harm to others. It is reasonable for a Supporter to be concerned that she, the Supporter, might be held financially responsible for her Consumer or her Consumer's actions.

There are situations where parents, children, and spouses will be financially responsible for each other. There are also situations where someone, related or not, might be responsible for another's actions. The general law on the subject of Supporters' responsibilities is set out below, broken up into the areas of tort liability, contractual liability, and government reimbursement.

Tort Liability

A tort is a legal wrong perpetrated by one person against another, usually outside of a contractual arrangement. The following are examples of torts: injuring another as a result of driving a car negligently, physically attacking someone, invading another's privacy, harassing someone, defaming someone. When harm is suffered as a result of another's tort, the injured person is entitled to be compensated for the harm. The harm might consist of money lost, or wages lost, or medical expense incurred, or the cost of an item lost or damaged, or emotional or physical harm (which can be hard to value, but definitely a type of harm for which the victim of most torts is entitled to be compensated).

A perpetrator of a tort, known as a tortfeasor, is financially responsible to the tort's victim. If compensation cannot be agreed upon, then the injured party can bring a legal action against the alleged tortfeasor. In such a lawsuit, the issues of whether a tort was perpetrated and if so, what the compensation should be, are submitted to a court for determination.

Usually, family members of a Consumer and other Supporters will not be automatically liable for a Consumer's tort. There are situations, though, where a family member or other Supporter will be held responsible to a Consumer's tort victim.

Where due to specific circumstances a Supporter has a duty to prevent a tort, and it is deemed possible for her to prevent the tort, and she fails to take steps to do so, she can be held responsible. An example is a parent of a Consumer who knows or should know that providing her child with a vehicle or a weapon poses an exceptional risk of danger due to the child's mental state or past actions. Giving this Consumer a vehicle or a weapon, or even just allowing the Consumer to possess them without taking any steps to take them away, such as reporting the possession to the police, could result in responsibility of the parent to a victim of the Consumer's use of the vehicle or weapon.

Similarly, where a Supporter is aware of a Consumer's dangerous propensities but fails to take any reasonably expected action to try to control the Consumer or to warn or protect a known potential victim, this would result in the Supporter's liability to the victim.

In these situations, the Supporter is actually not being held responsible for the Consumer's tort, but instead is being held responsible for the Supporter's own tort in enabling the Consumer to perpetrate a tort. It isn't only a parent who can be held liable. Anyone who provides a dangerous instrument such as a car or gun to one with known dangerous propensities, or who unreasonably fails to try to prevent a tort or warn a potential victim, is likewise subject to liability when the person knew or should have known of the Consumer's inability to safely use the dangerous instrument, or her propensity to harm another.

There is a specific type of liability imposed on parents who have custody and control of minors where someone is injured as a result of the minor's "willful misconduct."[48] This liability is limited, with the limitation changing bi-annually based on a cost of living index. The current limit is $45,000.00.[49] The parent's insurance company can only be held responsible for up to $10,000.00,[50] so there is personal exposure for a parent of up to the difference of $35,000.00. In defining willful misconduct, a California court of appeal decision has described it as an exaggerated form of negligence where one has intentionally done something which she knew or should have known would most probably result in harm to another.[51] In a situation where a minor Consumer might lack the capacity to appreciate that her conduct is actually misconduct, it is hoped that her misconduct would not be deemed "willful."

There is also liability imposed on a parent of a minor who drives with the parent's permission. In this situation the parent is automatically liable to a victim of the minor's negligent driving whether or not the parent had any knowledge of the minor ever being a negligent driver.[52]

---

[48] Civil Code section 1714.1
[49] California Rules of Court, Appendix B
[50] Civil Code section 1714.1(e)
[51] *New v. Consolidated Rock Products Co.* (1985) 171 C.A.3d 681
[52] Vehicle Code section 17708

There is also liability imposed on at least one parent of a minor even if the minor is not driving with the parent's permission. A minor cannot obtain a driver's license without one of her parents signing the application, and the signing of the application imposes liability on the parent signing it.[53] If a minor has a license, then at least one of her parents, *i.e.*, the parent who signed the driver's license application, will be liable for any damages caused by the negligent driving of the minor.

There is also a special type of liability imposed on owners of vehicles, who are liable for injuries caused by the driver of the vehicle regardless of familial relationship or age of the driver. There is a limitation on this type of liability of $15,000 per injured victim with a total limit of $30,000 per accident regardless of the number of victims.[54] This is unrelated to the liability that can ensue from a minor child negligently driving a vehicle with the parents' permission or from a parent's knowledge of a child's dangerous propensities. Those are separate areas of liability for parents, and ones without monetary limitations.

A child is not responsible for the torts of her parent unless due to circumstances the child had a duty to prevent a tort and failed to do so, *i.e.*, where the child provides the parent with the means to do damage with the knowledge of the parent's inability to safely avoid causing damage.

A spouse is not individually responsible for the torts of her spouse, but her share of "community property" can be taken by a tort victim who has obtained a court Judgment. This is because community property is liable for a spouse's tort.[55] Absent an agreement between spouses altering their property rights, community property consists of both spouses' earnings, and any assets purchased with those earnings. Each spouse is deemed to own one-half of all community property. So

---

[53] Vehicle Code section 17707
[54] Vehicle Code section 17151(a)
[55] Family Code section 1000

even though a spouse does not have personal liability for her spouse's torts, her one-half share of community property (along with the one-half share of the tortfeasor-spouse) is subject to being involuntarily used to satisfy a judgment against the other spouse. However, because the spouse is not individually liable, her separate property – those assets which she owned before marriage or acquired after marriage by gift, or are established as separate property by agreement between the spouses – is not subject to being used to pay a tort judgment against her spouse. There are numerous reasons for spouses to enter into agreements with each other altering community property rights, but to protect a spouse's share of community property from the victim of a tortfeasor-spouse, the agreement would likely need to be entered into before the liability-inducing act.

Contractual Liability

A parent is not responsible for her child's contractual obligations. If a Consumer signs a contract obligating her to pay money to another, she alone is responsible for paying the money. However, if a Supporter signs a contract obligating her to pay money to a provider of services or goods to a Consumer, whether the Consumer is her child or not, it is the Supporter who is the contractual obligor and who is financially responsible as such. Likewise, if a Supporter signs a contract as a guarantor of a Consumer's contractual obligations, then the Supporter is responsible for those obligations. In these situations of financial responsibility, the Supporter would be responsible due to her own promises, not due to her relationship to the Consumer.

A minor cannot be held financially responsible for contractual obligations since a minor has no legal ability to enter into a contract. If she purports to enter into a contract, neither she nor her parents would be liable under that invalid contract. A minor's parents would be liable to one who has provided the minor with necessaries of life, i.e., food, housing, or medical and dental care, either by reason of an invalid contract or otherwise.[56]

An adult child is not responsible for her parent's contractual obligations unless the child has signed the contract as a guarantor.

A spouse is individually responsible for necessaries of life provided to her spouse.[57] Again, necessaries of life consist of food, housing, and medical and dental care. Individual responsibility means that one's separate property and her share of community property are subject to being taken by another person who has acquired a court judgment against her spouse for necessaries of life.

A spouse is not individually responsible for the provision of items to her spouse which are not necessaries of life. However, absent an agreement between spouses altering their property rights, a spouse's share of community property is responsible for her spouse's contractual debts, even for non-necessaries.[58]

Governmental Reimbursement Rights

As shown in Chapter 5, there are numerous programs under which a governmental entity – city, county, state, federal – assists Consumers. To qualify for most of these programs a Consumer must display some degree of financial hardship. For eligibility purposes an adult Consumer's finances normally are considered independent of her family's finances. This means that one usually will qualify for public benefits if her family has wealth so long as she, herself, lacks sufficient assets and income and thus displays financial hardship. A question that concerns families is whether the governmental entity providing the benefits ever has a right of reimbursement from the family.

---

[56] Family Code section 3950
[57] Family Code section 914
[58] Family Code section 910

Questions frequently arise among Supporters as to whether benefits paid by the Social Security Administration and benefits paid by Medicaid are subject to reimbursement by a financially able family member. The answer is no, they do not have reimbursement rights against family members, regardless of financial ability. However, not all issues of governmental reimbursement by family members are as straightforward as Social Security and Medicaid.

Whether other government entities have a right of reimbursement from a Consumer's family members depends first on whether one has a legal duty to support the Consumer. If there is no legal duty to support a Consumer, then there would be no right of reimbursement. Where there is a legal duty to support a Consumer, a relative may or may not be liable for reimbursement to a governmental entity which provides that support.

Laws on the subject of governmental reimbursement rights are sometimes byzantine, and they differ in various ways from state to state. And even where governmental entities have a right of reimbursement, they do not always enforce this right. Following is the law of California.

Obligations of Parents

Parents are responsible for the support of their minor children (in California children under the age of 18). And if the state or county is supporting a minor child the state or county has a right of reimbursement from the parents.[59] The estate of a deceased parent of a minor child is also liable for support, and if the estate does not make provision for that support and the state or county is providing that support, then the state or county has a right of reimbursement from the estate.[60]

Where parents fail to support a minor child, the child or either parent or a county providing support can obtain a court order requiring

---

[59] Family Code section 3950
[60] Family Code section 3952

either or both of the parents to support the child.[61] And as said, if the county is supporting the child, then the county has a right of reimbursement from the parents who are able to support the child but are not doing so. However, this rule is not applicable to services provided by a county specifically as a result of disability, *i.e.*, parents are not liable for reimbursement to a governmental entity for social or rehabilitative services provided to their disabled minor children.[62] So if a county supports a child solely because the child's parents who have the ability to support her will not do so, then the county has a right of reimbursement from the parents. But if a county provides needed services solely due to the child's disability, then there is no right of reimbursement. The theory behind this rule is that parents generally have a legal duty to support and maintain their minor children, but they do not have a specific legal duty to pay for the cost of confinement, supervision, treatment, and rehabilitation of them when they have been separated from their parents for the benefit and protection of society.[63]

Parents of a minor child, or of an adult child claimed as a dependent on an income tax return, are liable to reimburse the state for Medicaid payments for the child.[64] They are also liable to reimburse a county which has made general relief payments to the child.[65]

Parents of an adult child also have a legal duty to support that child to the extent of the parents' ability if the child, due to incapacity, is unable to support herself.[66] As with a minor child, the child or either parent or a county providing support can obtain a court order requiring a parent with the ability to support the child to do so. However, neither the county nor the state has a right of reimbursement from the parents

---

[61] Family Code section 4001
[62] Welfare and Institutions Code section 12350
[63] *County of San Mateo vs. Dell J.* (1988) 46 C.3d 1236
[64] Welfare and Institutions Code section 14408
[65] Welfare and Institutions Code section 17300
[66] Family Code section 3910

for social and rehabilitative services provided by the county to a disabled child, adult or minor.[67]

There is no right of reimbursement on behalf of the state in a situation where an adult child is subject to an involuntary confinement in a state hospital or other institution due to mental illness. The California Court of Appeal held that the predecessor of California Welfare and Institutions Code section 7275, which allows such a right of reimbursement, arbitrarily and unfairly imposes obligations on specific classes of persons and is therefore unconstitutional and unenforceable.[68]

Obligations of Children

An adult child with the financial ability to support her needy parent has a legal duty to do so.[69] In fact, an adult child who has the ability and fails to support her needy parent actually commits a crime by that failure and is subject to imprisonment and fine.[70] (No record has been found evidencing a prosecution of anyone for the commission of this crime.)

A county does not have a right of reimbursement from a child for the social or rehabilitative services provided by the county to a disabled parent,[71] nor does the state have a right of reimbursement for what it provides.

There is no right of reimbursement on behalf of the state in a situation where a parent is subject to an involuntary confinement in a state hospital or other institution due to mental illness. The California Supreme Court held that the predecessor of California Welfare and Institutions Code section 7275, which allows such a right of reimbursement, arbitrarily and unfairly charges children of persons with

---

[67] Welfare and Institutions Code section 12350
[68] *Department of Mental Hygiene vs. Bank of* America (1970) 3 C.A.3d 949
[69] Family Code section 4400
[70] Penal Code section 270c
[71] Welfare and Institutions Code section 12350

mental illness and therefore violates both the United States Constitution and the California Constitution, and is unenforceable.[72]

Obligations of Spouses

Spouses have a legal duty to support each other.[73]

Where one fails to support her spouse who needs support, the unsupported spouse or a county providing support can obtain a court order requiring the spouse with financial ability to support her needy spouse. And if a county is supporting the needy spouse, then the county has a right of reimbursement from the other spouse who is able to support the needy spouse but is not doing so.[74] But like the situation with parents and children, a county which is providing a needy spouse services due to medical disability is not entitled to reimbursement for the social or rehabilitative services provided to the disabled spouse due to the disability.

Although as mentioned above, the state has no right of reimbursement from a parent or child of one institutionalized for mental illness under section 7275 of the California Welfare and Institutions Code, the state does have a right to obtain reimbursement from a spouse for a hospitalization of the other spouse.[75] The reasoning behind the court's holding that a spouse's liability under section 7275 of the Welfare and Institutions Code is constitutional is that a spouse has an obligation to support her spouse independent of that code section.[76]

Conclusion

In our legal system one is not generally responsible for financial liabilities of others. There are, however, numerous exceptions to the general rule,

---

[72] *Department of Mental Hygiene vs. Kirschner* (1964) 60 C.2d 716, and 62 C.2d 586
[73] Family Code section 4300
[74] Family Code section 4303; Welfare and Institutions Code section 17300
[75] Welfare and Institutions Code section 7275; *Department of Mental Hygiene vs. O'Connor* (1966) 246 C.A.2d 24, and *Department of Mental Hygiene vs. Kolts* (1966) 247 C.A.2d 154
[76] *In re Conservatorship of Edde* (2009) 173 C.A.4th 883

i.e., various ways in which one can find herself financially responsible for another person. The exceptions fall into two main categories: 1) where as a matter of law one is liable for the acts of another, and 2) where one voluntarily assumes liability for another. For the first category, there is little if anything we can do about potential liability, other than spouses entering into agreements altering their property rights *vis a vis* each other, which will provide some protection against creditors. We can protect against the second category by not voluntarily assuming obligations for others, although due to our Consumer's needs that is not always a practical solution.

CHAPTER 7

ESTATE PLANNING

Introduction

If there is anything more stressful for us than dealing with the mental illness of a loved one, it is dealing with it while contemplating our own death or incapacity. That we are mortal and thus at some point will become unable to help our loved one is one more aspect of the relentless reality of dealing with mental illness. It is crucial for Supporters to plan for the day when we will be unable to help our Consumer. The good news: there are effective ways to do this and doing it will reduce anxiety levels.

The two common concerns about future assistance to a Consumer are what happens if a Supporter becomes incapacitated to the point where she can no longer personally help the Consumer, and what happens when the Supporter dies. There is not a single way for all Supporters to provide for either of these eventualities, as there are endless differences between each Consumer's needs and between each Supporter's ability to help. The options will be presented below, along with explanations of the most common and necessary estate planning methods.

When a Supporter Becomes Incapacitated

Power of Attorney and Successor Trustee of Living Trust

Every Supporter should have a financial power of attorney as part of her estate plan. It will enable a person selected by the Supporter to handle financial affairs and transact business in the name of the Supporter should she become unable to do so herself. This includes paying bills and providing for financial needs. Financial powers of attorney are discussed in Chapter 1 and in Chapter 10; some pertinent parts are restated here.

Any adult can give to any other adult a financial power of attorney. It is done with the execution of a legal document in which the person giving the power, called the "principal," designates another, called the "agent," to make financial decisions and engage in financial transactions for her. A financial power of attorney can be "springing," in which case it only becomes effective upon the principal's incapacity, or it can be made "durable," meaning that the powers given are effective immediately and endure – remain in full force and effect – should the principal become incapacitated. Financial institutions and government agencies generally respect and accept a financial power of attorney, and this document will enable an agent to take care of business for the principal in ways she never could without it.

Power of attorney forms can be obtained online or in stationary stores, but because of the options available and the importance of getting all of it right, it is recommended that an attorney be hired, if not to draft one and have it executed, then at least to discuss it. Power of attorney forms often offer options to the persons signing them, and the document needs to be executed in conformance with the law of the state where it is signed. An attorney will be able to explain the options, and to have the document executed correctly, and this should not be too expensive. If it is done incorrectly it will likely be invalid and of no use, which might not be discovered until after the principal has become incapacitated, and at that point, due to the incapacity, she might be unable to execute a new and valid power of attorney.

When one becomes incapacitated and unable to handle her own finances, the agent named in the power of attorney is empowered to use the assets and income of the principal as the agent believes the principal would do herself. This means that where a Supporter has been assisting a Consumer financially, the Supporter's agent would act properly in continuing that assistance. The power of attorney could also be drafted so as to expressly provide for this.

A power of attorney is for assets that are titled in one's individual name. There will often be assets titled in the name of one's living trust. A living trust is commonly used in place of a will as a method of providing for after-death distributions of one's assets.

The advantage of a living trust is that the assets of the living trust are not required to be part of a probate court administration of a decedent's estate. Its assets and income can be used and distributed to its beneficiaries without court involvement. Staying out of court is economical. A living trust normally saves a lot of money – executor's fees, attorney's fees, and court costs – which would otherwise need to be spent on the extremely labor-intensive process of probate administration that might otherwise be required if there were no trust.

If there is a living trust, then the trustee or successor trustee named in it will have the power to use the assets and income of the trust for the purposes stated in the trust. Likely the same person who is named as the agent in a power of attorney should be named as successor trustee of a living trust.

Living trusts and wills will be discussed in more detail below under the section of planning for one's estate after death.

Planning for incapacity with a power of attorney and with a living trust is the most efficient and least expensive planning method available. As explained below there are other options. At least one of them is a good one (a special needs trust) and one of them should be avoided if possible (a conservatorship).

Special Needs Trust

Because a special needs trust is most frequently used as part of one's after-death asset distribution arrangement, it is discussed in detail below under the section of planning for one's estate after death. But to understand how a special needs trust can be used for planning in the case of a Supporter's incapacity, a few basics need to be understood.

A special needs trust is a specific type of trust which exists for the purpose of holding assets and using them for the benefit of a disabled person, usually one who is receiving public benefits, *i.e.*, a Consumer. The trust consists of a fund which is usually created by a Supporter, and which is then controlled and operated by the Supporter or someone else other than the Consumer. It exists solely for the Consumer's benefit. If structured correctly it will preserve the Consumer's public benefits while allowing the Consumer to receive financial benefits from earnings of the trust. It can take the place of a Supporter's personal financial assistance at any time, including the Supporter becoming incapacitated.

The requirements regarding the use of the trust's assets and income must be spelled out in the document creating the trust, and a trustee must be designated to operate the trust. The trustee will need to understand the Consumer's illness and specific needs, and also will need to know pertinent government program rules and how to avoid causing a loss of eligibility or benefits for the Consumer.

One can establish a special needs trust which becomes effective and operative immediately, or which becomes effective and operative only at some future time. Commonly a Supporter has no need to set up a special needs trust or to make one effective while she is able to provide needed assistance herself. She might be concerned, however, that the agent in her power of attorney and the successor trustee of her living trust will not necessarily provide the needed assistance after her incapacity. If she has this concern, then a special needs trust can be established immediately, and provisions made that it be funded and used after incapacity or death.

It is not necessarily a good option to establish a special needs trust for immediate use. This is because there is a financial cost to establish and operate it. Otherwise, though, it is a perfectly good way of accomplishing protection for a Consumer. One of its other benefits is that it efficiently enables persons other than the Supporter who establishes it to contribute to it without being required to establish their own special needs trusts within their own estate plans.

A note on the phrase, "special needs trust:" Because it is created for someone who is likely receiving public benefits, so as to provide funds for needs not paid for or provided by public benefits, it is often also called a "supplemental needs trust." For many, this other title is preferable, as it describes the reason for the trust as being a Consumer's supplemental needs without deeming them "special." Certainly "special needs" is not used to offend. People with disabilities do have needs that are special, and if a disabled person is impoverished to the extent that she needs public benefits, then it is accurate to call a trust established to supplement those benefits either a supplemental needs trust or a special needs trust. As "special needs trust" is so ingrained in the process and is not universally considered to be offensive, it is being used here.

Conservatorship

Probate conservatorships are discussed in detail in both Chapter 1 and Chapter 10. Establishing one for a Supporter will enable the conservator – the person who operates the conservatorship for the Supporter's benefit – to continue providing financial assistance to a Consumer. However, due to the large amount of time, work, and cost involved, a conservatorship is not an optimal way of accomplishing this. Essentially a conservatorship is a fall-back position, one taken only where a plan for incapacity has not been established or for some reason has failed.

In a probate conservatorship, a court will appoint a conservator for the incapacitated person, and the conservator will take charge of her assets. The court must approve of all expenditures made by the conservator. If the court is shown the history of the incapacitated person financially assisting a Consumer and is satisfied that she would want to continue assisting the Consumer and is also satisfied that there are adequate funds to use for the assistance, then the court will authorize it. In any event, though, the conservator would need to prepare and file an accounting with the court every two years, showing every expenditure made and obtaining the court's approval for each one.

When a Supporter Dies

There are various after death planning mechanism available as described below.

Will or Living Trust

Currently under California law,[77] assets titled solely in the name of a decedent which have a cumulative value in excess of $166,250.00 at the time of the decedent's death, must go through a probate court administration, *i.e.*, the assets must be "probated." This means the winding up of the decedent's financial affairs and the distribution of her assets must be overseen and approved by a court.

A will spells out what happens to assets titled in the name of a decedent after her death. Using a will is an orderly way of providing for distribution of assets after death, but again, will or no will, if the

---

[77] California Probate Code section 13100

decedent's individually owned assets have a cumulative value of more than $166,250.00 (in 2020), then they will need to be probated.

Because of the expense involved in a probate administration, it is often a good idea for Supporters to establish a living trust, and to transfer individually owned assets to this trust. This will result in the avoidance of probating these assets. A probate administration will not be needed if a Supporter is careful to keep less than $166,250.00 worth of her assets titled solely in her individual name, and this can be done if title to assets is put into a living trust.

The reason why a living trust will avoid probate is that assets will be owned by the trust, not by the Supporter individually. The document establishing the trust will set out how these assets are to be distributed.

The way a living trust works is that the person creating it – referred to interchangeably as the trustor, settlor, or grantor – transfers title of her assets from herself individually to her living trust. After the transfer the trustor is no longer the individual owner of the assets – the trust will have become the owner of them – and when the trustor dies those assets will not be subject to the law that requires probate of one's individually owned assets exceeding $166,250.00 in value. Instead, the after-death disposition of the assets will be controlled by the terms of the trust, and there should be no need for court supervision and its attendant costs.

Frequently ownership of some assets will be in the name of a living trust, and ownership of some will be in the decedent's individual name. If the individually-titled assets exceed $166,250.00 in value and do not on their title document provide for a payable-on-death beneficiary, those assets will need to be probated, and will necessitate the cost of a probate court administration. There may be assets titled in one's individual name that contain payable-on-death designations, and these will also escape probate administration, as explained below.

Both a will and a living trust are almost always revocable. This means the person who creates them can modify or terminate them at any time. Until death one can change her will or revocable trust any way she wants, including changing the after-death beneficiaries, or simply ending the existence of the will or trust. After death, both a will and a trust become irrevocable, meaning they cannot be changed or terminated, at least not without a court order under exceptional circumstances.

A will designates a personal representative to be in charge of individually owned assets after death. That person is called "the Executor" of the will. The document establishing the living trust typically designates the person creating it as the trustee, *i.e.*, the operator of the trust, who will be in charge of its assets, with a successor trustee named to be in charge after incapacity or death of the original trustee.

In her will or trust a Supporter would almost certainly want to establish a special needs trust for her Consumer which would go into existence after the death of the Supporter, or else provide for distribution to a special needs trust already in existence. (See below.)

If no estate plan is in place, and a decedent dies without making any provision for after-death distributions of her assets, and there are individually owned assets without payable-on-death beneficiaries in excess of $166,250.00, then those assets will need to go through a probate court administration. After expenses, the remaining assets of this probate estate will be distributed to those entitled to them under the law of intestate succession. The law of intestate succession provides that if one dies without a will or trust then at least a portion of her assets is to be distributed to her spouse, parents, siblings and/or children.

If one dies intestate, *i.e.*, with no estate plan in place, then of course no special needs trust will have been established to receive a distribution of assets. If there is a Consumer who would be entitled to at least a portion of the decedent's estate under the law of intestate succession, and who lacks the ability to protect her assets and/or would lose eligibility for public benefits upon personal receipt of the assets, then the court would likely need to order the establishment of a special needs trust to receive the Consumer's share. Such a court order would need to be specially applied for and the court persuaded that it is appropriate. It would have significant financial costs, and might contain provisions not wanted by the decedent, or possibly by anyone else. It is far better to intentionally create a special needs trust as part of an estate plan.

Special Needs Trust

For a Supporter, a special needs trust is the major element in protecting assets for a Consumer and preserving her public benefits – the crown jewel of the after-death estate planning process.

Like all trusts, a special needs trust is a legal entity that exists for the purpose of owning and controlling assets. The trust can be made revocable or irrevocable. If revocable, then the assets of the trust are deemed to belong to whomever has the right to revoke the trust. A revocable special needs trust might be advisable if done for other than after-death planning. It is not advisable for after-death planning as it is usually important that the trust not be subject to anyone else's right to terminate it. Sometimes, however, Supporters might want to include provisions in the trust that allow the termination of the trust and distribution of its assets to a Consumer upon conclusive evidence of the Consumer having recovered from her illness. It is also a good idea to give the trustee – the operator of the trust – the power to modify terms which might need modification due to new laws being enacted.

Like all trusts, a special needs trust needs a designated trustee. The trustee of a special needs trust will receive transfers of assets to the trust, and she will need to invest them prudently. The trustee will operate the trust for the sole benefit of the Consumer, who is called, "the trust beneficiary," and is designated as such by the deceased Supporter. The job of the trustee is usually not a simple one, and requires both financial skills and interpersonal skills, as well as knowledge of mental illness, a familiarity with the Consumer and her individual situation, and knowledge of the rules regarding payments for the benefit of one receiving public benefits.

The Trustee

Frequently the most significant and most difficult part of creating a special needs trust is the selection of the trustee. A trustee must be multi-talented. She must be able to invest trust funds safely, yet productively. She must be able to use trust funds effectively, yet without jeopardizing public benefits. She must be able to deal constructively with the trust beneficiary while being solely responsible for determining what type of expenditures are best to make. And she must try to maintain the trust funds so they will last for the life expectancy of the beneficiary.

Trustees come from the following groups: a trusted friend, relative, financial institutions, organizations operating pooled trusts, and private professional fiduciaries.

A Trusted Friend

There is little better in this world than a trusted friend, and when it comes to naming the trustee of a special needs trust, a trusted friend is often the best possible choice. That the person is a friend and is trusted says most of it. But this person still must have the talents described above in order to be a good trustee, and she also must have the willingness to take on the job and its responsibilities.

One downside of naming a trusted friend is the friend's mortality. An individual fiduciary does not have the built-in succession of an institutional or organizational trustee. When naming a friend as a trustee it is wise to not only name a successor trustee, but to give the named trustees and successor trustees the authority to name their own successors if that were to be needed. Succession is a key consideration, and most special needs trusts will not come into existence until the trustor is deceased and therefore unable to designate successor trustees when they would be needed.

A Relative

Relatives may feel a sense of obligation, which if based on love or a sense of duty can be quite good, and which if due to a sense of guilt can be quite bad. As with a trusted friend, the willingness and the talents are needed. And again, succession is an issue.

A Financial Institution

Banks and investment companies often maintain trust departments which manage clients' trusts, and many of them are willing to serve as trustees of special needs trusts. They tend to be expensive, so this type of trust might only make sense with a relatively large trust. A financial institution likely knows how to invest money, and almost surely it would hire a case manager and possibly other professionals to interact with the beneficiary on a regular basis, and to report to the trust department so it will know what expenses to pay for. Financial institutions will want to review trust provisions and possibly include some of their own before agreeing to serve as a trustee of a special needs trust, and arrangements for that should be made before making the designation of one as a trustee.

Despite their capitalization requirements, financial institutions do go bankrupt. If trust funds are segregated as legally required, and properly invested for maximum protection, then a special needs trust should survive an institution's bankruptcy unscathed.

An Organization That Operates a Pooled Trust

There are organizations that exist for the purpose of serving as trustees of special needs trusts. They exist under laws that allow them to pool their trust assets for investment purposes, and each of them have established its own master special needs trust so that its language controls all of the trust estates that the organization administers. These organizations are specialists, set up to do this job, and are likely do it in a professional way.

Sometimes these organizations will contract with personal support professionals or case managers, and the organization will know what makes one of them better at her job than another.

These organizations can be expensive, although sometimes they will contract with Supporters to receive a percentage of the funds remaining in a special needs trust at the death of the beneficiary, which may enable them to make their ongoing charges more reasonable. One caveat here is that if an organization operating a pooled trust were to lose assets because of negligence or embezzlement, then it might be harder for a successor trustee to recover them for the trust than it would be if this occurred with a financial institution and its likely higher capitalization. But if the organization maintains insurance to cover such losses, then recovery of lost assets might not be an issue at all.

A Private Professional Fiduciary

In California one can be certified by the state as a private professional fiduciary, *i.e.*, one who for a fee handles money belonging to someone else. To qualify for certification, an individual must show skill, knowledge and experience in handling finances, have a history of trustworthy behavior, and post a performance bond with the state to insure against defalcations. Many private professional fiduciaries serve as trustees of special needs trusts, and due to a familiarity with mental illness and its victims that comes with their experience, they are sometimes able to do so without the assistance of a hired case manager. A private professional fiduciary can be an excellent choice as trustee, but there is a downside, which is, as it is with naming a friend or relative, the mortality of the individual fiduciary. Naming successors is absolutely necessary

Use of Trust Funds

The governing document which establishes a special needs trust will specify what expenses can and cannot be paid for with trust funds. It may also specify what expenses *should* be paid for. The decision on how to actually use trust funds, however, needs to belong solely to the trustee, who will exercise her own discretion on this. The beneficiary, on the other hand, must never have the ability to control assets or income, or direct what is to be paid for by the trustee, as this would invalidate the special needs trust provisions.

The trustee needs to have knowledge of the rules surrounding whatever government programs the trust beneficiary is enrolled in, so that she can be sure not to jeopardize eligibility or cause a loss of benefits. If SSI eligibility is a factor, as it usually is, then the trustee must be aware that there are potential adverse ramifications if trust funds are given to a Consumer or if trust funds are used to pay for housing or food. For example, cash payments to a Consumer in excess of $20.00/month reduce SSI monthly payments by one dollar for every dollar paid until the point of ineligibility is reached. Payments for housing and food will also reduce the amount of the monthly SSI payments, although in a more limited amount. A full explanation of the SSI rules, and the consequences of paying for housing or food, is contained in Chapter 5. The trustee must be cognizant of the SSI rules, and must be willing and able to stay up to date on them because they do change from time to time.

Complicating the job of the trustee of a special needs trust is the need to maintain the existence of the trust for the expected lifetime of the beneficiary. The reality of most special needs trusts is that there is not going to be any other fund available to supplement the Consumer's public benefits, and if a special needs trust spends all of its money there is no way to replenish it. So, the trustee must continuously keep a running approximation of the Consumer's life expectancy, and of the length of time the trust assets will continue to exist at current rates of investments and expenditures. And of course, the trustee must try to keep the investment rate of return on trust assets at a high level while keeping the risk of loss on investments at a low level.

Effective Date of Trust

A special needs trust can be established by a Supporter's living trust or will and become effective only upon incapacity or death of the Supporter. This is the most common way it is done.

A special needs trust can also be created by a separate document, to be effective immediately or upon some future event such as the Supporter becoming incapacitated or dying. This option is usually employed when it is anticipated that there will be various sources of funding. For example, if a parent is going to establish a special needs trust for the benefit of her child, and she recognizes that the child's other parent or another relative or a friend will likely be making a future gift to the child, then likely she would be concerned about the additional cost and possible confusion caused by the establishment of a separate special needs trust. This parent might want to establish one trust, effective immediately, inform the other potential donors of its existence, and ask that they make their future gifts to this trust instead of creating a new one. The success of this project might be dependent on who the trustee of the trust is. If a Supporter is going to create a trust effective immediately so that the trust will be able to receive future gifts from others, the Supporter is advised to try to ensure that the choice of trustee is agreeable to the other prospective contributors.

Duration of Trust

Typically, a special needs trust is established for the life of the beneficiary, although it can be set up so that it will terminate sooner. Some Supporters will include provisions in the establishing document that call for the distribution of trust assets to the beneficiary if it is independently determined that the beneficiary is forever recovered from her illness and no longer needs to have her inheritance controlled by a trustee. This independent determination frequently consists of at least one declaration made by a treating psychiatrist. It should be noted, though, that unless an irreversible cure for mental illness is developed, it is not always realistic to expect that such a declaration could be obtained.

Disposition of Trust Assets After the Beneficiary's Death

The document establishing a special needs trust must specify what is to be done with the remaining trust assets at the death of the beneficiary. Usually provision will be made for the payment of outstanding expenses and taxes, for expenses of disposition of the beneficiary's remains, and for administration expenses, with the balance then to be distributed to whomever the Supporter wants to receive it. Again, it would invalidate the special needs trust provisions if the beneficiary had any control over the assets, and it is an open question whether control of after-death distributions would constitute this prohibited "control." To be safe, the final distributions should not be dependent on any selections being made by the beneficiary.

It is important to understand that the trust assets are never owned by the trust beneficiary, and that neither the beneficiary's creditors nor governmental entities ever attain any right to the trust assets. The Social Security Administration has no reimbursement rights against the trust for money paid to the beneficiary, and states have no reimbursement rights against the trust for Medicaid payments made for the beneficiary. This follows from the fact that the trust assets came from the Supporter and then are owned by the irrevocable special needs trust, and these assets are never owned by the trust beneficiary. The assets belong to the trust, not to the beneficiary of the trust, and no one claiming against or through the beneficiary has any right to those assets.

Income Taxation

If a special needs trust is irrevocable, which it normally will be after the death of the person establishing it, then it will become a taxpaying entity at the time it becomes irrevocable. As such it will need to obtain a taxpayer identification number from the Internal Revenue Service and use that number for all of its investments and holdings, and on its tax returns. An irrevocable trust is required to file income tax returns and pay income tax. A potential financial burden to the use of an irrevocable special needs trust is that its income, consisting of returns on its investments, is taxable at a higher rate than the rates for individuals earning income with their investments. However, there is also a potential benefit, which is that the trust may also qualify for an increased exemption amount not available to individual taxpayers if it is deemed a "qualified disability trust" (QDT).[78] This can prove to be significant. The requirements for a special needs trust to qualify as a QDT with its increased exemption are as follows:

1) The trust is a "nongrantor" trust. To understand this, we first need to understand that in addition to all of the other types of things that trusts can be, they can also be either grantor trusts or nongrantor trusts. The difference is that due to the wording used in a grantor trust, someone other than the trust itself is responsible for the taxes assessed on its income. This could be the grantor, *i.e.*, the person who creates the trust (also known as the "trustor" or "settlor"), or it could be the beneficiary. With a nongrantor trust it is the trust itself that is responsible to pay any income taxes. An irrevocable special needs trust created by a Supporter for a Consumer's benefit is almost always a nongrantor trust.

2) The trust is irrevocable. Again, this means it cannot be modified once it comes into existence.

3) The trust is established for a disabled person who is under 65 years old.

Many special needs trusts created as part of a Supporter's estate plan will qualify as QDTs and have higher exemptions than individual taxpayers.

---

[78] Internal Revenue Code section 642(b)(2)(C)(ii); 42 USC section 1396p(c)(2)(B)(iv)

Summary

If public benefits are not an issue, and protection of assets is the only concern, then instead of creating a special needs trust, a Supporter could make a gift of assets to a non-special needs trust for the benefit of the beneficiary. This would enable the trustee to make distributions such as, cash payments to the beneficiary including periodic payments to her. It could still provide protection for the trust assets, but it would not preserve public benefits. The only way to enable a Consumer/beneficiary to qualify or remain qualified for public benefits is to establish a special needs trust. As public benefits are an issue for the vast majority of Consumers, it is usually necessary to establish a special needs trust to receive distribution of assets on behalf of a Consumer.

Payable on Death Designations

Retirement accounts – IRAs, 401Ks, etc. – must be titled in the name of the individual who establishes them and are not to be owned by that person's living trust. So long as these accounts designate after-death beneficiaries they do not need to go through a probate court administration. It is therefore crucial that this designation take place when one establishes a retirement account, or at some other time before death. In the case of a Supporter who wants the account to be used after her death for the benefit of a Consumer, it is crucial that either a special needs trust be named as the after-death beneficiary, or that a living trust be named if that living trust has special needs trust provisions for distributions benefitting the Consumer.

There are numerous laws and rules pertaining to retirement accounts which affect the ability of the account beneficiary to continue operating the retirement account after the original owner's death. These laws and rules affect who can be named as eventual beneficiaries of the account. An in-depth explanation of them here is not feasible. If retirement accounts are going to be set up so that they are to be distributed even in part to a special needs trust, then it will be necessary to consult with an attorney knowledgeable on this subject before it is done.

Non-retirement accounts at financial institutions, and real property (land and buildings on land) which are titled in one's individual name, can be set up so they become payable on death to a designated beneficiary. This would exclude them from probate. The need to have a special needs trust or a revocable living trust designated as the payable-on-death beneficiary would exist for these assets as well, so that a Consumer does not end up individually owning an asset which she may not be able to handle, and which will disqualify her from public benefits.

When a Consumer Inherits Outright

Not all Supporters' estates are perfectly planned out. Sometimes a Supporter's will or living trust makes a gift directly to a Consumer. And sometimes Supporters die without a will or trust and their assets are then distributed by a court pursuant to the law of intestate succession.

If a gift is made directly to a Consumer, or if a Consumer is entitled to receive assets under the law of intestate succession, then the Consumer likely is going to be facing a loss of public benefits. As more fully explained in Chapter 5, one is eligible for SSI and Medicaid only if her assets have a value of less than $2,000.00.

Even if a Consumer is not receiving SSI or Medicaid, there would be a significant problem if the Consumer does not have the ability to personally handle the inherited assets.

Where a Consumer inherits assets outright, there are various options available to safeguard the inheritance and to preserve public benefits. All of them are explained in Chapter 9.

Conclusion

Planning our estates is as important as most everything else we do for a Consumer. The estate planning should be done with careful thought, and with the advice of a knowledgeable attorney. If it is not done, or not done correctly, there are often ways to remedy the situation, but it will have become a problem. And while it is frequently a solvable problem, the solution is usually expensive. Best to get it done when alive and well.

CHAPTER 8

ABLE ACCOUNTS

Introduction

An Achieving a Better Life Experience (ABLE) account is a type of financial cash account which can be established by a disabled person or her representative in accordance with Federal law.[79]

The main purpose of an ABLE account is to enable a Consumer or her representative to maintain a bank account without the use of the funds in the account adversely affecting the Consumer's Social Security Supplemental Security Income (SSI) or Medicaid benefits. Money in an ABLE account is allowed to be used for many things including daily living expenses and housing, without it causing a reduction of SSI or Medicaid. An added benefit of an ABLE account is that account earnings are not subject to income tax.

An ABLE account is set up through a state-run program. Each state can offer ABLE accounts, but the state must first establish rules and procedures and make necessary arrangements to implement the law. At the present time not all states have implemented the law. However, regardless of where a Consumer is residing, an ABLE account can be

---

[79] Internal Revenue Code section 529A(e)(5)

opened in any state that has implemented the law. Opening an ABLE account can be done without the need to hire a lawyer, but a lawyer's advice before opening the account should be sought.

Rules Applicable to ABLE Accounts

The law allowing ABLE accounts (see footnote 1) establishes specific rules for setting up and operating them. And the Social Security Administration has established additional rules to govern operation of these accounts as they affect a Consumer's ability to qualify for SSI.[80] Following is a summary of the law and its rules, and the Social Security rules, as applicable to ABLE accounts[81]:

1) An ABLE account can only exist for a Consumer whose onset of mental illness was before age 26.

2) The account can be opened and operated by a Consumer or by a Consumer's authorized agent, trustee, or custodian. An authorized agent includes an agent under a power of attorney executed by a Consumer. A trustee includes a trustee of a special needs trust in existence for the benefit of a Consumer. The account can hold only money, and no other assets.

3) There is a limit as to how much funding can occur each year, and that limit is equal to the amount of money that can be gifted by an individual to any other individual without the donor having to file a federal gift tax return. Currently this amount is $15,000.00 per year. This is a cumulative limit, meaning contributions to an ABLE account from all sources cannot exceed $15,000.00 per year. However, if a Consumer is working and earning wages, she can make additional contributions, solely from her wages, of up to $12,140.00 per year, which means she

---

[80] Social Security Program Operations Manual System (POMS) SI 01130.740.

[81] Although an attempt is made to explain these laws and rules in a simplified, straightforward manner, they are labyrinthine, and readers might expect to still find them confusing.

could have total contributions to her ABLE account of $27,140.00 in any one year.

4) Only one account per Consumer is allowed. Currently the limit that an ABLE account can hold without the account affecting the Consumer's SSI is $102,000.00 less whatever SSI "countable resources" the Consumer might have. (Countable resources are the assets owned by a Consumer which Social Security considers in determining financial eligibility for SSI; see Chapter 5) So, *e.g.*, if a Consumer's countable resources have a value equal to the maximum SSI limit of $2,000.00, then she can have no more than $100,000.00 in an ABLE account. If the balance goes over that there will be a suspension of payments of SSI. There is no limit on the amount in an ABLE account with respect to food stamps or Medicaid eligibility, *i.e.*, the amount on deposit in an ABLE account does not affect food stamps or Medicaid eligibility or benefits.

5) To prevent reduction of SSI, taxation of the account's earnings, and a financial penalty, the money in the account must be used only for what the law calls, "qualified disability expenses." A qualified disability expense is defined as a distribution which is related to the account owner's disability and is made for her benefit. There are numerous items which would constitute a qualified disability expense, including housing, transportation, medical expense, personal and financial support services, education, legal fees, and expenses for funeral and disposition of remains. It appears the only things that might not constitute a qualified disability expense are food purchases, cash distributions to the account owner, or gifts to others. And food, although not specifically listed, is an open question, since expenses for basic living expenses and health are deemed to be qualified disability expenses, and food should fit into either of those categories. Good record keeping is required to support the use of the money should an audit occur.

6) On the Consumer's death the balance in the account is subject to Medicaid reimbursement rights, like a d4A first party special needs trust (see Chapter 9), unless the State entitled to reimbursement chooses not to seek it.[82]

As said above, the existence of an ABLE account will not affect SSI eligibility if the balance in it plus the value of all countable resources is under $102,000.00, and it will not affect Medicaid eligibility regardless of how much the account balance is. But there is a question whether a Consumer can make herself eligible for public benefits or retain her eligibility by transferring her own money to an ABLE account.

Say a Consumer has a non-ABLE bank account with a balance of $10,000.00. She would be ineligible for SSI due to her countable resources being over $2,000.00. If she were to transfer that $10,000.00 to an ABLE account, it would constitute a transfer of resources without consideration (in essence a gift), and such a transfer normally will not allow one to qualify for SSI. To accomplish eligibility in that situation, a spenddown or a first party special needs trust would normally be needed. (See Chapter 9.) But one of the purposes of an ABLE account is to enable an SSI recipient to retain SSI eligibility, and the ABLE account law specifically allows the account holder to transfer up to $15,000.00 per year to the account. And an ABLE account has the same Medicaid payback provisions (see below) as a first party special needs trust that does enable qualification for, or continuation of, SSI eligibility. Because of this it is believed by many that an ABLE account can receive a transfer of countable resources from a Consumer in order to qualify the Consumer, or to continue her eligibility, for SSI. However, there would be a risk in doing this, as Social Security might conclude that since there is nothing in the ABLE law or rules that specifically says one can transfer

---

[82] As set out in the rules it established to implement the ABLE law, California has chosen not to seek reimbursement from an ABLE account on the Consumer's death for Medicaid paid on behalf of the Consumer.

her own countable resources to an ABLE account to qualify or continue eligibility for SSI, it is therefore, not allowed.

If an ABLE account is not operated correctly, there would likely be at least some loss of public benefits, as well as income tax imposed on account earnings and a penalty. Specifically, if disbursements from the account are deemed improper and then disallowed by the Internal Revenue Service, then there would be a 10% penalty plus income tax imposed on the distributions, along with whatever adverse consequences that would likely ensue with SSI.

Benefits of ABLE Accounts

An ABLE account can be especially good for a high functioning Consumer, as it will enable her to control her own money. She can even be issued a debit card so that she can use the account for purchases. If operated correctly, it will supplement public benefits, and there will be no income tax on the account's earnings.

If an SSI recipient were to receive a windfall of $15,000.00 or less, then to remain qualified for SSI (see Chapter 9) she might be able to transfer the money into an ABLE account, although this is not entirely clear. (See discussion above.) If allowed, a transfer to an ABLE account might be an attractive alternative to establishing a first party special needs trust or spending the money down to below $2,000.00 in order to qualify, or to remain qualified, for SSI.

The limit of $15,000.00 per year for contributions as well as the maximum limit of $102,000.00 for the total account balance for SSI recipients seriously restrict the ability to use an ABLE account, either while a Supporter is living or as part of an estate plan. Certainly, an ABLE account will not replace all financial assistance that can be provided by a Supporter or by a special needs trust (see Chapters 7 and 9 for explanations of special needs trusts). But an ABLE account can be used in conjunction with a Supporter's assistance or with a special needs trust, as shown below.

A Consumer or her agent could set up an ABLE account, and a Supporter or the trustee of a special needs trust for the Consumer could fund it at a rate of up to $15,000/year. Then, all or part of the money contributed each year to the ABLE account could be used for the Consumer's housing expenses. This would provide a benefit for the Consumer who is receiving SSI, because payments for housing which are made from an ABLE account will not have any effect on the Consumer's monthly SSI stipend. If these funds were paid for housing directly from a Supporter or from a special needs trust, SSI would be reduced. (See Chapters 5 and 7.) In this ABLE account scenario, the Supporter or the special needs trust would not be directly spending $15,000.00 on housing, but instead would distribute that money to the ABLE account, and the ABLE account would then spend it on housing. It seems like a bit of money of laundering, but it is perfectly legal, and would benefit a Consumer on SSI.

Also, if the ABLE account were established while a contributing Supporter is living, and if the ABLE account were not then needed to help with housing costs for a Consumer on SSI, then the Supporter could make annual maximum contributions to the account until the balance reached the maximum of $102,000.00. Then, after the death of the Supporter, a special needs trust established by the Supporter could come into operation. At that point, if the Consumer were to need help with housing, the ABLE account would have enough money in it to pay more than $15,000.00/year for housing. The special needs trust could then continue to fund the ABLE account at the rate of up to $15,000.00/year and replenish at least part of the money used by the ABLE account for housing.

As shown, if a Supporter is assisting a Consumer on SSI with housing payments, then it likely would be to a Consumer's advantage for an ABLE account to be established. It would necessarily depend on the housing costs, and the amount of money that is available for the Consumer's needs.

Conclusion

An ABLE account can be set up and operated by a Consumer or by her authorized agent or trustee. If the amount of funds in the account will not adversely affect the Consumer's SSI, i.e., if it is less than $102,000.00 when combined with the Consumer's other countable resources, and the Consumer is able to handle the funds in the account, then an ABLE account would be superior to, or would at least be a good adjunct to a special needs trust. This is because 1) the Consumer would be in charge of her own money, 2) the ABLE account would not require the cost of hiring a trustee, 3) the account could be used for housing without adversely affecting SSI, and 4) there would be no income tax on the account's earnings. Even if the Consumer is not able to handle the account herself, and an agent is required to operate it for her, if the agent is the trustee of her special needs trust, there shouldn't be too much extra work for the agent, and likely not a substantial additional cost. Although there is income tax savings by use of an ABLE account because income earned in an ABLE account is not taxable, income tax savings alone may not be enough to make it profitable to establish an ABLE account.

It seems the rules applicable to an ABLE account are more complex than they ought to be for an account which is so restricted in the amount it can hold and the annual amount that can be contributed to it, and for its overall narrow benefits. But along with its limitations, and with the risks if not operated correctly, an ABLE account definitely can have benefits and be worthwhile. An ABLE is not for everyone, but it can be good for some.

CHAPTER 9

PROTECTING ASSETS AND PRESERVING PUBLIC BENEFITS AFTER A WINDFALL

Introduction

A Consumer might receive a financial windfall. It might be an inheritance or a gift which is made directly to her instead of being made to a special needs trust for her benefit. Or it might be a Judgment or settlement based on a legal claim, which results in payments directly to her. Or she might be designated a beneficiary of a contract between others, and as a result of that she could receive cash or other assets.

As more fully explained in Chapter 5, to qualify for SSI or Medicaid, or to remain qualified, a Consumer cannot hold title to most liquid assets of $2,000.00 or more. So, if she receives a windfall which increases those assets to more than $2,000.00, and she needs to qualify or remain qualified for SSI or Medicaid, then she is going to need to divest herself of the windfall, or at least that portion of it which when added to her existing liquid assets totals more than $2,000.00 in value. The ways to safeguard the windfall and to either qualify for or to preserve public benefits are explained below.

Options for Safeguarding the Assets and Preserving Public Benefits

Giving Away the Windfall

Giving away assets might benefit a Consumer if it enabled the donee of them to use them for the Consumer's needs and keep the Consumer qualified for public benefits. The general rule is that one cannot give away assets in order to qualify, or remain qualified, for public benefits.

Sometimes people think this rule can be avoided if the Consumer signs a disclaimer in which she relinquishes the right to receive the windfall. This will not solve the problem, however, as a disclaimer itself is deemed a giving away of the assets disclaimed.

There are two exceptions to the rule preventing the giving away of a windfall. One is when a Consumer makes a transfer of the assets received to a self-settled special needs trust. This type of trust is fully explained below.

The other exception is a limited one, and exists when a Consumer qualifies for Medi-Cal independently of SSI, *i.e.*, the qualification for Medi-Cal is not based on SSI eligibility. One who qualifies for SSI automatically qualifies for Medi-Cal, but one can qualify for Medi-Cal independently of SSI.

If a Consumer is receiving SSI and Medicaid, and she gives away (most) assets, she will be disqualified for SSI and Medicaid for up to 36 months, depending on the value of the assets given away. But if she has qualified for Medi-Cal separately from SSI, she will still maintain eligibility for a type of Medi-Cal.

There is a type of Medi-Cal called "community" Medi-Cal. Community Medi-Cal pays for medical care, including doctors, medications, and hospitalizations. Non-community Medi-Cal, on the other hand, pays for long-term care services, including nursing home charges. One who qualifies independently for Medi-Cal, *i.e.*, not through SSI, and who gives away a windfall to reduce her assets below the $2,000.00 threshold, will continue to qualify for community Medi-Cal.

Giving away assets to qualify for community Medi-Cal might be impracticable. A Consumer might need long-term care services in the future and if she has given away assets then she may not qualify for non-community Medi-Cal in the future to pay for the long-term care services. Also, there is no provision in the law that protects assets given away from Medi-Cal recovery claims, *i.e.*, Medi-Cal has a right to reimbursement for certain payments it has made if a Medi-Cal recipient acquires disqualifying assets exceeding $2,000.00 and giving away such assets might be treated by Medi-Cal as a violation of its recovery rights

Spending Down the Windfall

While a Consumer may not be able to give away the windfall, she can use it for her needs and actually spend enough of it so that the total value of all of her assets is less than $2,000.00. In essence, she would be converting the windfall from cash to goods and services. This may not be a good solution where the windfall is large, because it would mean virtually all of it must be spent and would not be available for future needs. With a relatively small windfall, however, it is often the best solution. It depends, of course, on what items might be needed by the Consumer.

A valid spend-down requires arms-length purchases for fair market value. This means the items purchased must be worth what is being paid for them. So, *e.g.*, if a Consumer uses $50,000.00 to purchase a 10-year-old car with 150,000 miles on it and which is nowhere close to being a collector's item, then she has not validly spent down that money because the purchase was not for fair market value. If the actual value of that purchased car is say, $3,000, then anything over $3,000 likely would be treated as exceeding fair market value, and would be deemed a gift by the Consumer to the seller. Which means the attempted spend-down would likely fail, since generally one cannot give away assets in order to qualify for public benefits.

Most items purchased for fair market value will be deemed exempt assets, meaning that ownership of them will not disqualify a Consumer from public benefits. There are some items – essentially those that are liquid assets – which will not be deemed exempt. *E.G.*, purchases of an annuity or of a cash value life insurance policy or of a certificate of deposit or of stocks or bonds would not be valid spend-down purchases since those are items which can be readily converted to cash.

One might question why an item such as an automobile or a computer or a couch or a television will be deemed an exempt asset since it can be sold and thus converted to cash. The difference between investments in financial assets and consumer items seems to be 1) consumer items can be used for the immediate benefit of the Consumer instead of solely being an investment so as to earn money in the future; and 2) the consumer item normally would not be deemed an investment at all, due to it typically losing value over time instead of having the potential to gain value. Given that the purpose of SSI and Medicaid is to provide poor people with food, housing and medical care, the government does have an interest in not making grants of money to and paying medical bills for people who have more money than what they need for basic living expenses.

A disqualification based on the value of assets received would begin only in the calendar month following receipt of the windfall. It is deemed to be *income* during the calendar month of receipt and does not become an *asset* until the following month. So, if the spend-down is made so as to reduce the Consumer's liquid assets to below $2,000.00 during the calendar month of receipt of the windfall, then the value of the windfall would not adversely affect eligibility for public benefits. But as it would be deemed income during the month of receipt, it still could disqualify the Consumer during the month of receipt based on monthly income limitations.

Below are some common spend-down options.

Payment of Debts

Paying debts is a legitimate and often good way to spend down. The debt should have some objective form of proof. *E.G.*, a credit card debt can be established with an invoice from the bank which issued the debt. But a debt to a Consumer's sibling without anything evidencing it other than oral statements saying the debt is owed due to previous undocumented loans would have a strong chance of being disapproved by the government agencies in charge of the public benefits for which a Consumer is trying to gain or retain eligibility. Record keeping is important, as is a promissory note or receipt or cancelled check which shows the actual loan and consequent debt.

Prepayment for Services and Other Items

A prepayment for the cost of future services or goods can be a valid spend-down payment. A typical example of this is a contract entered into by a Consumer where a person agrees to provide things like food and shelter or personal assistance over a period of months or even years in exchange for a lump sum payment made at the time the contract is entered into. SSI rules expressly allow a personal services contract which will last for the Consumer's life. The key to success is for the Consumer not to pay so much for the goods or services that a government agency would be apt to make a determination that the purchase was for less than fair market value.

There is a distinct downside to prepaying for food or shelter: there would be no future cost to factor into the Consumer's expenses for the months that have been prepaid. Which means that SSI might be reduced due to lower living expenses in those future months.

There are other downsides to prepaying for services or goods. The money paid by the Consumer will be income to the recipient of it, and taxed as such during the year of receipt. This could result in a larger income tax for the person who provides the services or sells the goods.

Another potential problem of prepaying for personal services is that performance of the contract might become impossible due to illness or death of the other party (usually a caregiver), or abandonment by the other party, or a change in the Consumer's circumstances. These risks must be considered in determining the specifics of a personal services contract, including the amount paid for the services by the Consumer.

A personal services contract would require specific provisions, including the actual services or service categories to be provided, and under what circumstances the services will be provided. The contract should be drafted by an attorney

Creating and Funding a Special Needs Trust

There are types of special needs trusts that can help, as described below.

Court-established Special Needs Trust

In a situation where a decedent leaves assets to a Consumer outright, courts can come to the rescue by creating a special needs trust to receive and use the assets inherited. (See Chapter 7 for an explanation of special needs trusts.) In order to obtain a court order establishing the trust there would need to be a petition filed with the court showing either that 1) the decedent was unaware of the Consumer's mental illness; 2) that although cognizant of the Consumer's illness, the decedent was not aware of a way to provide for the Consumer other than by outright gift; or 3) that upon learning of the illness or learning of the availability of a special needs trust, the decedent was unable to make the needed changes in her estate planning documents.

In the situation where a Consumer receives assets by will or by intestate succession, there may be an existing court proceeding in which the court can be petitioned to establish a special needs trust to receive the distributions to which the Consumer is entitled. In that situation the petition would be part of an existing court action, and it should be a little easier to accomplish, and the cost should be a little less, than if a new court action were required.

If a court will not grant this petition and create the special needs trust, or if it is not feasible to petition the court, then often the best way to deal with the potential loss of public benefits where a spend-down will not work is with what is known as a self-settled, or 1st party special needs trust.

Self-settled Special Needs Trust

A self-settled trust is a type of special needs trust which is created by or for a Consumer. One of its distinguishing characteristics is that it is funded with the Consumer's own assets. Because the source of funding is an individual's own assets, it is referred to as a 1st party trust, which differentiates it from a trust created and funded by someone else, which is referred to as a 3rd party trust. A self-settled (or 1st party) trust will protect a Consumer's assets in most situations, qualifying the Consumer or keeping her qualified for public benefits. There are limitations to using this type of trust.

One limitation is that usually a Consumer must agree to it, as the assets to be transferred to the trust are assets which either she owns, or she is entitled to own. Because it means she would give up control of her assets, she might not agree to it.

Another limitation of a self-settled special needs trust, or at least a possible drawback, is that on the Consumer's death any assets remaining in the trust must first be used to reimburse the state for Medicaid payments to the Consumer.

There is a type of self-settled special needs trust that consists of joining what is called a *pooled trust* (see below). If the Consumer agrees that assets remaining in this trust at the Consumer's death are to be retained by the organizational trustee which operates the trust, then the assets will not need to be reimbursed to the state for its Medicaid payments.

Either way, if the Consumer has family or friends or others who she would want to receive all of the trust assets on her death, there are these impediments to that occurring with a self-settled trust.

It is important to understand that although there are Medicaid reimbursement rights against assets of a 1st party special needs trust, there are none against assets of a 3rd party special needs trust. That is because the assets belonged to a 3rd party before they were transferred to the trust, and the Consumer/trust beneficiary never owned those assets. (See Chapter 7 for a full explanation of 3rd party special needs trusts.) Medicaid reimbursement rights are allowed against a self-settled trust because the trust has been funded with the Consumer's own assets, not with a 3rd party's assets. It is true that with a windfall situation the assets recently belonged to a 3rd party, but at the time the 1st party special needs trust is created those assets or the right to receive them are owned by the Consumer and would otherwise disqualify the Consumer from SSI or Medicaid. As such, the assets are subject to Medicaid reimbursement. This is one reason why a court-ordered special needs trust might be a superior method of dealing with a windfall, since a court-ordered special needs trust usually takes the form of an amendment to a 3rd party's estate plan, and thus it establishes a 3rd party trust against which the state has no right of reimbursement for Medicaid payments.

It is also important to understand that if a windfall that would disqualify a Consumer from public benefits is transferred to a self-settled trust, thus preserving the Consumer's public benefits, the state would have a future reimbursement right for Medicaid paid for the Consumer not just after age 55 (see Chapter 5), but for Medicaid paid at any age, and at any time.[83] The theory, which is a sound one, is that a Consumer is being allowed to make herself qualified for Medicaid by transferring her own assets to a self-settled trust, and so assets remaining in the trust on its termination should be available for all Medicaid reimbursement just as it was before being transferred to the trust.

A self-settled or 1st party trust is funded by a Consumer. It can be established by its beneficiary, *i.e.*, the Consumer, or by authorized persons such as parents or guardians of the beneficiary. The trust comes in two separate types.

In one type of 1st party trust, the person creating the trust designates a trustee in the establishing document. Because of the law allowing these trusts[84] they are frequently referred to as *d4A trusts*, and due to the Medicaid reimbursement requirements, they are also referred to as *payback trusts*. As discussed below, a d4A trust is not available for a Consumer who is 65 or older.

The other type of 1st party trust is where a Consumer joins a pooled trust, which is a master special needs trust operated by a nonprofit organization for the purpose of pooling together assets of disabled persons for investments. The organization that operates a pooled trust is often also referred to (inaccurately and confusedly) as a pooled trust. This organization serves as the trustee, managing the special needs trust and following the rules pertaining to the use of trust funds for a Consumer. To join, a Consumer contracts with the organization.   Due to the law allowing pooled trusts,[85] they are frequently referred to as *d4C trusts*.

The chief differences between a d4A trust and a d4C trust are as follows: 1) there can be investment advantages of pooling assets in a d4C trust (economies of scale); 2) if she wants to, the Consumer can direct after-death disposition of trust assets to the organization

---

[83]Social Security POMS SI 01120.203(B)(1)(h)
[84] 42 USC section 1396p(d)(4)(A)
[85] 42 USC section 1396p(d)(4)(C)

operating the d4C trust, and the state would only receive Medicaid reimbursement from any assets not distributed to that organization; 3) a d4C trust likely will have a professional trustee, and likely would employ a professional investment adviser, which means decisions should be well thought out; 4) a d4A trust is not allowed for a person who is 65 or older, making the d4C trust the only potential self-settled trust option for this Consumer.

Even though the law does not allow a transfer of individually owned assets by a Consumer who is 65 or older to a d4A trust in order to qualify her, or to keep her qualified for SSI or Medicaid, a d4A trust which was established before the Consumer reached 65 is still valid and its assets are still deemed not to be owned by the Consumer once she reaches the age of 65. But a d4A trust cannot be established for a Consumer who is already 65 or older, nor can assets be transferred from any source to an existing d4A trust after the Consumer has turned 65, without the Consumer's rights to public benefits being adversely affected.

For a Consumer who is 65 or older, a d4C trust (a pooled trust) is likewise not available to protect SSI, but it is a way to protect Medi-Cal eligibility, albeit in a limited way. Specifically, one who is 65 or over can establish and fund a new d4C trust and qualify or remain qualified for Medi-Cal – both community Medi-Cal which pays for medical care, and non-community Medi-Cal which pays for long-term care services, including nursing home charges. However, the limitation here is that non-community Medi-Cal will not be available after additional payments are made to a d4C trust which has already been funded at least once. I.E., a d4C trust can be set up and funded for a Consumer who is 65 or older, and enable her to continue receiving Medi-Cal, but if augmentation occurs by more funds being transferred to it, this would disqualify her from non-community Medi-Cal. So if a 65 year old Consumer who has established a d4C trust to receive her windfall should receive another windfall, or another installment on her initial windfall, she would need to establish another, separate d4C trust to receive the new money in order to stay qualified for non-community Medi-Cal. Extreme caution should be used in doing this, as allowance of this process is not written into the Medi-Cal law, and instead is the way that the California Department of Health Care Services (DHCS), which operates Medi-Cal, interprets the law. Thus, it is DHCS policy, subject to change, with a new and different interpretation always a possibility. Caution should also be used for Medicaid-eligible Consumers in states other than California, as this is a specific California application of the rules and this may or may not exist in other states.

Decanting to a Special Needs Trust

Sometimes a Consumer is designated the beneficiary of the income or principal of a trust upon the occurrence of some event such as the previous trust beneficiary's death. This might arise as part of an estate plan put together by spouses who want to provide for a child or other person after the deaths of the spouses. If they have provided in their estate plan for gifts directly to a person, who later develops a mental illness, once one of them dies it will be too late to completely change the gift.

A typical situation where this occurs is when the estate plan of spouses provides that on the death of the first spouse to die, the share of the deceased spouse in the spouses' assets is left in an irrevocable trust for the benefit of the surviving spouse for life, and then on her death whatever is left of it goes to others. This after-death irrevocable trust is often referred to as an *Exemption Trust, Bypass Trust, Credit Shelter Trust,* or *Trust B,* and the surviving spouse is often its designated trustee. When the first death occurs, this irrevocable trust is created, and being irrevocable, it cannot be changed. If a Consumer who is to receive distribution from this irrevocable trust after the death of the surviving spouse develops a disabling mental illness in the time between the death of the first spouse to die and the death of the second spouse to die, the surviving spouse can establish a special needs trust for the Consumer to receive any distributions from the surviving spouse's assets. But the surviving spouse can only provide for, make changes to the distribution of her share of the former marital assets. The share of the former marital assets which belonged to the deceased spouse would at that point already be owned by the irrevocable trust, and payable directly to the Consumer on the surviving spouse's death.

In this situation, a procedure exists under the law of decanting[86] that allows the trustee of the irrevocable trust to distribute the Consumer's interest to a special needs trust for the benefit of the Consumer.

This procedure is called *decanting*, as though the assets contained in one bottle (the irrevocable trust originally established) were being poured into a new bottle (an irrevocable special needs trust). It can occur without a court proceeding, and it will work in the example set out above and it will also work where a Consumer is a beneficiary of only income from a trust, as the trustee of that trust would be allowed to distribute the income to a special needs trust for the Consumer. The decanting procedure must be employed in strict accordance with the decanting law, and one of its crucial requirements is a notice given to interested persons explaining what is being proposed and giving them 60 days to file a court action if they object. Like all potential procedures in this chapter, this one should only be done by an experienced attorney.

An ABLE Account

An ABLE account may be a legitimate way to protect up to (currently) $15,000.00 per year. Its operation has many requirements. (See Chapter 8 for a full discussion of ABLE accounts and their requirements and uses.)

It is believed by some that an ABLE account can be used to receive a transfer of assets from an individual in order to qualify her for public benefits. The law does not specifically say that, but the law does

---

[86] Probate Code section 19513

effectively say that one can own an ABLE account with $102,000.00 in it without losing SSI eligibility, and funding by the Consumer herself is allowed. The law also says that any money remaining in an ABLE account at its owner's death may be subject to Medicaid reimbursement. Since Medicaid reimbursement is a factor in the law allowing a transfer to a 1st party special needs trust without the transfer being treated as a gift that would disqualify one from public benefits, there is a reason why a transfer to an ABLE account should be allowed without it being treated as a gift which disqualifies one from public benefits. The problem is that nowhere in the law or the rules is it written that one can transfer funds to an ABLE account in order to make herself eligible for public benefits. In any event, the transfer would be limited to $15,000.00 per year.

Conservatorship

A conservatorship, explained in Chapter 10, is an expensive and time-consuming proceeding that should always be avoided if at all possible. Sometimes, such as where a Consumer is fully incapacitated, there is no other option available, and a conservatorship is required to preserve both the windfall and the Consumer's eligibility for public benefits.

Lose Benefits

If a windfall is large enough, a loss of public benefits may not pose a problem. However, even if a Consumer no longer needs a monthly SSI stipend, she may still need a payment source such as Medicaid for ongoing medical care. And even if the cost of ongoing medical expense is affordable, there is still the present or potential problem of a Consumer being unable to handle the newly owned assets and making bad decisions in spending them. In these situations, a trust or a conservatorship would need to be established to receive the windfall.

Conclusion

Windfalls are wonderful, and likely no one during rational moments has ever objected to being the recipient of one. But for a Consumer who is dependent on public benefits and who might not be able to handle ownership of assets, something must be done to protect these assets and the Consumer's public benefits. In this situation, it is likely necessary to explore all of the available options set out in this chapter.

CHAPTER 10

AUTHORITY TO ACT FOR A CONSUMER

Introduction

Frequently it is necessary for a Supporter to act on behalf of a Consumer in a formal manner. As discussed in Chapter 1, when dealing with financial institutions, creditors, government agencies, or medical personnel, some badge of authority may be required before a Supporter can get cooperation. If a Consumer is able and willing to sign a consent form, that will usually constitute an acceptable form of authority. But if she is unable or unwilling to do so, then something else would be needed. That something else normally consists of either a power of attorney or a probate conservatorship.

Power of Attorney

When one executes a power of attorney she empowers an agent to act on her behalf. Powers of attorney can exist for financial matters and for medical decisions. A more thorough discussion of powers of attorney is contained in Chapter 1, and they are also mentioned in Chapter 7. They are important enough to mention again here.

There are forms for powers of attorney that can be obtained online. Since there are many different types of powers of attorney, depending on what they are needed for and the state where they are needed, and because preparation of a power of attorney is something that an attorney should be able to do for a relatively small fee, it is best if an attorney is consulted when one is needed.

It is recommended that a Supporter obtain both a power of attorney for finances and a power of attorney to make medical decisions (two separate documents in California) signed by a Consumer during a period of time when a Consumer is disposed to signing them, and not wait until they are actually needed before requesting them from the Consumer. It is frequently a decompensation – a radical worsening of a Consumer's mental condition – that necessitates action by a Supporter and the situation where the Supporter might be required to show her legal authority to act. During a period of decompensation, a Consumer will likely be confused, and as a result she might be unwilling to give such authority to a Supporter. If a power of attorney has already been executed and in place, and if the power was given in such a way as to be "durable," which means that it is to remain in effect if the person giving the power becomes incapacitated, then the Supporter will be able to act on behalf of the Consumer.

A Consumer who has executed a power of attorney has the power to nullify it, but for that to happen the Consumer would need to display the capacity to understand what she was doing, and in a state of decompensation she may no longer have that capacity. Possibly, even if she had the capacity, her confused state might result in her not being cognizant of the fact that she previously provided an agent with a power of attorney, or that she has the ability to nullify it. If not nullified, it would provide the named agent with legal authority to act on behalf of the Consumer. So even though a Consumer would have the power to later terminate a power of attorney, she should still be encouraged to execute one when she is able and willing to do so.

If a Consumer will not execute a power of attorney, or if she has terminated it, or if she refuses to sign a separate authorizing document presented to her by an authority requiring it, then a probate conservatorship might be required.

Probate Conservatorship

A probate conservatorship is a type of court proceeding where a court will issue formal orders bestowing authority on one person to make decisions for another who lacks the capacity to make her own decisions. There is a similar court proceeding known as a guardianship which exists for the benefit of a minor who has no able parent. The procedures are sometimes similar; it is a conservatorship which might be needed for an adult Consumer and will be explained here.

As noted in Chapter 1, California has two basic types of conservatorships – a probate conservatorship and a Lanterman-Petris-Short Act (LPS) conservatorship. An LPS conservatorship exists for the situations where an involuntary hospitalization is required and is fully explained in Chapter 2. If what is desired is authority to act for another short of committing her to a locked psychiatric unit, and she will not execute a power of attorney, then it is a probate conservatorship that would be needed.

A probate conservatorship is complex and difficult to institute and operate, and it is labor-intensive for courts and attorneys and therefore expensive. Because of the complexities and the cost, a conservatorship is generally an inferior method of establishing authority for another and should be used as a last resort. But if there is no power of attorney in existence, and something more than a transitory or interim need for authority exists, then a conservatorship may be the only available option.

In California each county's court system has a probate department, and it is responsible for cases involving the rights and assets of persons who lack capacity to care for themselves and their assets. These cases are called probate conservatorships.

Probate conservatorships are divided into estate conservatorships and personal conservatorships.

Estate Conservatorship

An estate conservatorship is formally known as a *Conservatorship of the Estate*. "Estate" refers to one's financial assets and financial transactions, and an estate conservatorship can be applied for in order to protect one's assets and to transact her financial affairs. The power of a conservator of the estate, which is the title given to the person who pursuant to a court order operates an estate conservatorship, is analogous to the power of one who has been given a financial power of attorney. The difference is that a conservator is appointed by the court and is subject to court supervision over all she does.

An estate conservator has the power and duty to take control of the assets of one who lacks capacity to adequately control them herself – the conservatee – and the conservator must protect those assets and use them for the sole benefit of the conservatee. As the conservator assumes the power of handling financial matters for the conservatee, she must post an insurance bond with the court unless excused by the court from doing so. The bond will serve as a source of funds to replace the assets of the conservatorship were the conservator to wrongfully take them or lose them in some careless way. The court supervises all that is done by a conservator, and the conservator must periodically (biannually in California) file an accounting with the court showing each transaction engaged in by the conservator for the conservatorship during that accounting period. The accounting must list every check written by date, payee, and purpose. A court investigator will periodically visit the conservatee and review the work done in the conservatorship, and report to the court on the continuing necessity of the conservatorship and its proper operation. A judge will then determine if all has been done right and if it should continue to be done in the same manner. A conservator can also apply to the court for orders allowing actions to be taken before actually taking them.

As readily seen, court supervision can create burdens for a conservator, not the least of which is the cost of compliance. The burdens are warranted where one is unsure of the ability of a conservator to faithfully carry out her duties. That is not necessarily the usual case, but court supervision is required in all conservatorships.

Personal Conservatorship

A personal conservatorship, formally known as a *Conservatorship of the Person*, can be established for one who is incapacitated to the point of being unable to make rational decisions about personal matters. Typically, these matters involve her living situation and her medical needs. The personal conservator's powers are somewhat similar in scope to those of one who has been given a power of attorney for medical decisions; a personal conservatorship will enable the conservator to communicate with medical providers.

What a personal conservatorship will not do, just as a medical power of attorney will not do, is enable the conservator to place a conservatee in a locked psychiatric unit against her will. An LPS conservatorship (see above, and see Chapter 2) is required to accomplish that.

Due to the limited scope of a personal conservatorship, it is somewhat easier to maintain than an estate conservatorship. But a personal conservatorship also is labor-intensive and expensive, and also should be avoided by using a power of attorney when possible.

The Probate Conservatorship Process

A probate conservatorship starts with a petition filed with the court, requesting either a personal conservatorship or an estate conservatorship, or both. The proposed conservator does not need to be the petitioner, although she usually is. Anyone can file the petition, but spouses and relatives have priority to be appointed the conservator over all other persons. The petition sets out the facts which establish a need for conservatorship. Upon filing, the court will schedule the petition for hearing, and the person filing it – called the *petitioner* – will be required to have the proposed conservatee personally served with the petition and a notice of the hearing. Usually a medical professional's affidavit is required to be filed to establish the incapacity of the proposed conservatee. This affidavit typically consists of a court-approved form filled out and signed by the medical professional. Due to adherence of medical professionals to privacy laws, a court order directing a medical professional to provide an affidavit might be required. The court may appoint an attorney to represent the proposed conservatee if she does not have her own attorney. Another attorney of course adds to the cost, but it ensures that the conservatee's position, if contrary to the petitioner's position, will be heard, and it sometimes can help the conservatee understand the proceeding and appreciate that it is for her benefit and therefore not something to necessarily contest. If a conservatee does contest a petition, she is entitled to a trial on the issue of whether a conservatorship is required, another safeguard, also expensive.

Conservatorships require a substantial amount of legal work, including the need for court orders to perform various functions, with each petition for an order requiring a court hearing. The attorneys' fees, court fees, and other miscellaneous fees of conservatorships make them expensive.

A probate conservatorship will exist for the life of the conservatee, or until it is otherwise no longer needed. It can only be terminated with a court order, and that done only after a petition has been filed with the court requesting the order and showing the need for termination. The court is intimately involved with its conservatorships, and all that a conservator does must satisfy the court.

Conclusion

There will be times where a power of attorney for making financial decisions and/or a power of attorney for making medical decisions will be needed to provide a Supporter with authority to act on behalf of a Consumer. They should cost relatively little to establish. If possible, both of these powers should be obtained from a Consumer while she is in a rational state. They will remain effective unless and until they are revoked, or until for whatever reason one who is requiring a Supporter's authority refuses to honor them.

A probate conservatorship is an effective way to empower one to act on behalf of a Consumer who is incapacitated. It provides ultimate protection for the Consumer. It is also labor-intensive and expensive, but it does provide the imprimatur of a court order, and the protection of a bond, and court supervision to ensure all is done correctly. When a Supporter needs to act on behalf of a Consumer and can only do so with some form of authorization, and the Consumer will not cooperate, then a conservatorship may be the only option available.

CHAPTER 11

CONSUMERS' FINANCIAL OBLIGATIONS

Introduction

Like everyone else, Consumers tend to incur debt, often more so.

The laws which apply to debtors and creditors in general, and the procedures pertaining to enforcement of financial obligations fill volumes. It is neither possible nor desirable to list or even summarize all of them here, as so many have no bearing on issues specific to the Mental Health Community. The most common situations affecting Consumers involve contracts which bind them to pay for goods or services they neither need nor can afford, and it is these contracts that are discussed below.

Legal Issues Pertaining to Consumers' Finances

Contract Formation

Commerce is transacted through the use of contracts. Contracts are agreements – promises given in exchange for each other. One person or entity, who in contract law is called a party, agrees to provide an item or a service to another party who in turn agrees to pay for it. Both parties are then legally obligated to perform their promises.

A contract can be in writing. Or it can be oral. Or it can arise from circumstances. All three types are legally binding and enforceable.

The first type, a written contract, consists of an agreement that is in a writing that spells out the obligations of the parties to it, and also contains the signatures of the parties. A written contract is usually required by sellers and/or buyers for more expensive goods and services, *e.g.*, a purchase or rental of a home, car, phone, T.V., computer purchases and service, gym membership, insurance, and loans, including credit cards. The respective obligations of the parties to a written contract are spelled out in writing, and then signed by the parties.

The second type of contract, an oral contract, occurs when parties do not sign a written contract but do verbally express an agreement. An example is a lawyer saying to a prospective client that the lawyer will do specific work for a specific fee, and the client saying that's fine, what information do you need from me. A contract has been formed by those words; the attorney is bound to perform her promise to do the needed work for the stated fee, and the client is bound to perform her promise to cooperate and to pay the fee for the work.

The third type of contract, a contract that arises from circumstances, is sometimes called an implied in law or implied in fact contract. It doesn't require a writing or an oral expression, and instead it occurs when circumstances lead one to believe that legal obligations are being incurred. An example is when one gives her car to a parking lot attendant next to a sign that says what it costs to park there. At that moment the owner of the lot and the driver have entered into a contract by impliedly agreeing to perform certain implied actions for the benefit of the other.

Capacity to Contract

To be legally bound by a contract, either written, oral, or arising from circumstances, one must have the capacity to understand the nature and terms of the contract. If a party to a contract lacks this capacity, then no valid contract could be entered into, and any purported contract would be void. For this to occur it would need to be shown that a party did not understand a key portion of the purported contract, and that this was due to the party's lack of capacity to understand it.

Capacity to understand a contract is the crucial element. A Consumer can still be a party to a contract when she does not understand all of its terms or its full nature and extent, *i.e.*, it is not required that a party to a contract understand every single term of the contract. Most people, whether they suffer from a disabling mental illness or not, tend to bind themselves by contracts which they don't fully understand. It is when a party is unable to understand key provisions, provisions which are so substantial that without them there would be no purpose to the contract, that the contract can be voided.

It is usually a key provision that a party to a contract is trying to enforce. If there is a lease that requires a tenant to make monthly payments of rent and to provide a property insurance policy, it is likely the rent that is the key provision. The fact that the tenant might not precisely understand what the insurance provision requires would not help her in resisting enforcement of the lease due to a nonpayment of rent.

Whether one has the capacity to understand a contract is always a factual issue, and the person who wants to void the contract has the burden of establishing her inability to understand it. The worse that one's symptoms are, the greater the chance that she lacks capacity, and the better the chance of establishing incapacity.

Sometimes it can be obvious just from the nature of the contract that the person purporting to contract lacks capacity. If a Consumer residing in Des Moines, Iowa contracts online for a one-year membership with a fitness studio doing business only in Hartford, Connecticut, it is evident that the Consumer did not understand the nature of the contract, and it should not be overly difficult to persuade the studio to cancel it. Not all bad contracts are so clearly misunderstood, and persuading companies to void a profit-making contract is not usually easy.

Undue Influence and Fraud

There is another type of situation where a contract entered into by a Consumer can be voided, even if she had the capacity to understand it. This occurs when a Consumer is subjected to what is called, "undue influence." In this situation, a Consumer might understand the nature of the contract, but she doesn't understand that she has been taken advantage of by someone who has used her illness-induced vulnerability against her. Say there is a Consumer who lets another person live with her while the Consumer pays all of the rent and utilities and buys all of the food. Possibly the Consumer was in need of companionship and this arrangement, which is in fact a contract, was entered into to fill that need, which means it might have been to the Consumer's benefit to enter into it. But let's say the other person uses the home to entertain her friends, while excluding the Consumer from her get-togethers. In this situation, where the Consumer might not be getting the sought-after companionship from the transaction, then possibly the Consumer has been misled by the would-be companion. Perhaps the would-be companion saw the Consumer's susceptibility to her prospective companionship as a way to live cheaply and persuaded the Consumer that it would be to the Consumer's benefit to enter into this contract. If the other person occupied a position of trust with the Consumer, *i.e.*, if the Consumer looked to her for guidance or good decision-making, then the other person has exerted undue influence. And when the terms of a contract entered into by a Consumer as a result of undue influence are so onerous as to be deemed unconscionable, then that contract can be voided.

CONSUMERS' FINANCIAL OBLIGATIONS

Fraud is an intentional misrepresentation made to induce another to give up something of value. If a promise in a contract is in fact fraudulent, then the contract will be deemed void. The example given above for undue influence would also constitute a fraud. Fraud can be similar to undue influence, or different, but either way, a valid contract cannot be based on it.

When and How to Void a Contract

A contract entered into by one lacking capacity to understand it, or by one who is a victim of undue influence or fraud, is a voidable contract. This means that the contract can be extinguished, and the parties can have whatever they have given to the other for less than value returned to them, or if that is not possible, then cash that equals the value of what was given. But a voidable contract has to be voided by a party; it isn't automatic. Voiding can occur when one party prevails upon the other to agree to this, or when a court orders it.

When it is necessary to void a contract, a Supporter likely will need to act. How to act will be dependent on the situation. Sometimes it takes only a single phone call for a Supporter to void a contract entered into by a Consumer. Sometimes an attorney needs to get involved. Sometimes governmental authorities need to get involved. And sometimes it is not going to be possible to void a contract no matter who is involved.

Situations vary, but usually if a Supporter believes a contract was entered into by a Consumer who lacked the capacity to understand it or was the victim of undue influence, then the Supporter should probably start by contacting the other party to the contract and explaining the situation. Sometimes the need for an attorney can almost be guaranteed, such as where a Consumer has purchased a new automobile, has taken title to the car, and has driven the car; if that contract were voided, the seller would be left with a used car with a considerably lower value than what that car sells for new. But this is not to say that a car seller would never agree to void the contract, *e.g.*, if there were an inflated sales price

141

for a new car there might be enough profit in the payments made for the seller of the new car to absorb the reduction in value resulting from voiding a contract. These situations stand on their own, *i.e.*, each one is different and the results of efforts to void the contracts will also be different. The need for negotiations is likely.

Another time an attorney is needed is when a lender has engaged in what is called *predatory lending*. Predatory lending is characterized by unfair loan terms, the exploitation of a borrower's lack of understanding of loans and their terms, and risk-based pricing where a bad credit risk is charged inflated interest and penalties. Loans of this type are illegal under federal law and under the law of most states. Loaning money to a Consumer who has neither the ability to repay the loan or to fully understand the obligation will qualify as predatory lending.

Sometimes, such as when a roommate or another with an intimate relationship with a Consumer is unwanted, the County office frequently known as *Adult Protective Services* needs to get involved. The office of Adult Protective Services exists to protect and provide remedies for adults who cannot protect themselves and who tend to get victimized because of this. It will usually investigate complaints and use its immense governmental powers to remedy wrongs when found.

A good rule of thumb is that the more unconscionable the terms of a contract are for a Consumer, the more likely it is that the contract can be voided, either for lack of capacity or for undue influence or for fraud.

Compensation from a Wrongdoer

Sometimes a contract can be voided, but there has been wrongdoing on the part of the other party to the contract which results in financial or other injury suffered by a Consumer. The Consumer may be entitled to not only void the contract, but also to compensation for this. There are laws that enable victims of wrongdoing to be made whole, and also provide for penalties to be paid by a wrongdoer who has acted with ill will. In order to determine if a right to compensation exists, and how to obtain it, consultation with an attorney would be required.

Conclusion

When a Consumer enters into a contract without understanding it, and it is harmful to her, then action likely needs to be taken to void the contract. Not all bad contracts are subject to voiding, but often little is lost by trying to void one. Sometimes it is going to be necessary to consult an attorney or to engage government authorities, and in that situation a Supporter is going to need to decide whether it will be worth the cost in money, time and effort.

It is always worth noting that a contract entered into by a Consumer is potentially voidable if the Consumer lacked capacity to understand it or was subjected to undue influence or fraud as a result of her incapacity to understand the other party's motives. Just because one is the victim of mental illness does not mean that she must also be the victim of others' greed or malice or self-centeredness. Remedies are available, and sometimes they include compensation.

CHAPTER 12

RIGHTS AND OBLIGATIONS RELATED TO HOUSING AND EMPLOYMENT

Introduction

There are numerous laws governing housing and employment which pertain to Consumers. It would not be practical or necessary to try to include all of them in this book. However, there are two basic and important rules concerning housing and employment which most of us do need to understand, and they are included, and explained below.

The Right to be Free of Invidious Discrimination

Generalizations exist, and some are negative. There are owners of residential rental units and there are employers who prefer not to rent to or hire members of a group when negative generalizations exist about the group's members. This occurs when a generalization exists suggesting group members would be poor tenants or employees.

With regard to Consumers as tenants, negative group generalizations might consist of Consumers being less likely than others to pay rent timely, or more likely to make noise, or more likely to cause ambulance or police visits. With regard to Consumers as employees, negative group generalizations might consist of Consumers being less likely than others to arrive on time, or more likely to leave early, or more likely to bother other employees. These generalizations might be accurate, or not, but if a landlord or employer believes they are accurate, then she might conclude that it is in her best interest not to rent to or hire any Consumers at all.

Such a landlord or employer who discriminates against all Consumers based on what might be true of some Consumers likely sees herself as someone who is paying attention to behaviors and information and using common sense by playing the percentages in not subjecting herself to potential problems by renting to or employing people whose group characteristics indicate a greater likelihood of future difficulties.

A problem with this "common sense" approach is that even if the generalization that more Consumers than non-Consumers cause difficulties is statistically accurate, the resulting discrimination against *all* Consumers is unfair. Every Consumer should have the right to be judged on her own behavior, and not pre-judged and denied rights available to the rest of the public solely because of the past behavior of *other* Consumers. And in fact, under the law, every Consumer does have the right to be judged on her own behavior.

It might be tempting for a property owner to make a decision not to rent a home to a Consumer, or to try to charge her extra rent, due to a belief that because she is a Consumer there is a greater likelihood that she will be a worse tenant than a non-Consumer. The property owner might be able to present cogent reasons to justify her belief that persons with mental illness are more apt to lose the ability to pay rent or more apt to disturb other tenants. But whether or not these beliefs are in fact accurate, they would never be relevant to a Consumer's right to be treated as an individual, as opposed to being treated simply as a member of a group. If a Consumer displays a financial ability to pay rent when due, an ability to care for her home, and a respect for the rights of fellow tenants, then she should not be, and legally cannot be, denied housing because she has a mental illness.

The same is true with respect to employment. If a Consumer is qualified for a job through her education and work skills and whatever social abilities are needed for the job, and if she displays the required knowledge and intelligence and ability to get along with others and to be committed to timely finishing a job, then she should not be, and legally cannot be, denied a job because she has a mental illness.

Some people might think that the law should allow landlords and employers to play the percentages, and if it is more likely that Consumers will turn out to be worse tenants or worse employees than non-Consumers, then being denied housing or a job is just more tough luck for those Consumers who would be good or better tenants or employees. Even Consumers and Supporters can adopt this attitude. A simple analysis of how such discrimination might work against involuntary members of other groups should disabuse everyone of this attitude.

A far greater percentage of male drivers than female drivers get speeding tickets, get convicted of reckless driving and of drunk driving, cause vehicle accidents, and injure and kill people with their vehicles. These are statistical facts. So, should the state only issue driver's licenses to females? Discriminating in this way against all males would result in less disruption, injury and death, and a lesser number of ruined lives. This discrimination would thus provide distinct benefits to society. But it would also unfairly penalize good male drivers because of what other male drivers have done, and unfairly deny the safe drivers a basic privilege simply because of a random outcome of birth.

Discrimination is the act of discriminating, and as such it is not necessarily bad. In fact, it is frequently part of an intelligently lived life. Every time we make a choice we have discriminated against what we didn't choose, and that is often smart. But to discriminate against and penalize individuals based on nothing more than their involuntary classification is not to make an intelligent decision; it is to engage in a bad form of discrimination known as *bigotry*.

Actions based on bigotry exclude entire classes of persons from things the rest of the public can enjoy. Exclusion is due solely to a class of persons having immutable characteristics (ones that cannot be changed), which involuntarily place each person in this discriminated-against class. Mental illness is an immutable characteristic, and it puts its members into a discriminated-against class.

Actions based on bigotry unfairly deprive its victims of rights enjoyed by others, and as such is deemed to be offensive, even odious. The law calls this type of discrimination, "invidious." When invidious discrimination against Consumers occurs in a commercial setting, *i.e.*, when one is denied commercial advantages available to the rest of the public solely due to class membership, it is illegal.

It should be understood that people who wish to avoid dealing with mental illness are allowed to discriminate against Consumers in strictly personal affairs. These people can choose not to be friends with Consumers, or if they are friends with Consumers they can put limits on the friendship, such as not inviting the Consumers into their homes. These decisions might be due to bigotry, or not, and either way they might be hurtful to the Consumer discriminated against. But there is no legal obligation to be friends with anyone, nor is there a legal right for one to be welcomed into another's life. Association with others in non-commercial or non-public activities is usually the result of a personal preference and our society places enough value on this freedom that we don't disrespect and violate it by forcing people to give up discrimination in their personal affairs, no matter how invidious, absurd, or hurtful it might be. If someone wants to limit who she entertains in her home that is her absolute right. She can exclude persons with various immutable characteristics and in doing so perhaps exhibit bigoted animosities towards them, but the exclusion is tolerable in a free society because it allows people to exercise personal preferences that do not deny to the persons discriminated against any rights to public advantages shared by everyone else.

Lawmakers have recognized that humans are complex beings, and that individuals are far more than involuntary members of some group. Every person has her own genetic makeup, her own ancestral and environmental influences, her own personal code of conduct and ethics and intelligence and desires. Recognizing this, laws have been established to prevent individuals from being denied valuable things like housing and employment because of the possibility that a disproportionately greater percentage of persons sharing an immutable characteristic with them might prove to be problematic tenants or employees.

Equal treatment of persons who are involuntary members of a group is mandated by both Federal law[87] and the laws of various states.[88] These laws go beyond just a requirement of equal treatment; they require "reasonable accommodations" to be made for disabled persons who need them. If a Consumer requires an adjustment or modification of the rules such as being allowed the accompaniment of a companion animal in her home or being allowed to take extra breaks at work, then she is entitled to have a determination made as to whether such an accommodation is a reasonable one. Reasonableness necessarily turns on the degree of need experienced by a Consumer, and the degree of burden that would be experienced by a landlord or employer. When a landlord or employer cannot reach agreement with a Consumer on what is a reasonable accommodation, then there are government offices and courts which will decide that issue.

When violations of these rights can be proven, a Consumer injured by them is entitled to compensation from the wrongdoer.

---

[87] 42 U.S.C. section 3601 *et seq* (housing); and 42 U.S.C. section 12111 *et seq* (employment)
[88] In California, Government Code section 12920 *et seq* (housing) and section 12940(a) (employment), and Civil Code section 51 (all commercial transactions)

Property owners and employers tend to know this, and it provides incentive to the bigots among them not to invidiously discriminate. But of course, it still goes on, and when it does it may be necessary for a Consumer to hire an attorney to prove the violation and the appropriate amount of compensation.

Consumers' Obligations as Tenants and Employees

As said, a Consumer has the right to be treated fairly in her applications for a home and a job, and she has the right to receive reasonable accommodations too. But there are obligations that accompany these rights.

With housing, a Consumer has the same obligations as other tenants, such as paying rent fully and timely, caring for her home, respecting the rights of fellow tenants, and refraining from committing nuisances. And although a Consumer might be entitled to reasonable accommodations due to her illness, she can find herself lawfully evicted for violating tenants' obligations just as other tenants can.

As regards employment, Consumers, just like other employees, must perform their job duties and must not engage in behavior that reasonably disturbs fellow employees or the employer or its customers. Those who cannot fulfill these obligations will legitimately find themselves out of a job.

A Consumer who has been evicted from her home or fired from her job is likely going to have those past acts legally used against her by a new prospective landlord or employer. While mental illness is not something which a landlord or employer can use to deny anyone housing or employment, prior problems with landlords or employers can be legally used to deny one housing or employment. The fact that the illness might have been a cause of the prior problem is irrelevant. Here the Consumer is not being treated differently than a non-Consumer merely because she is a Consumer; she is being treated differently because of her own past actions. It is not legal to treat someone unfairly because she has a mental illness or any other immutable characteristic, but because one has a mental illness does not give her a free ride to commit bad acts.

There is an exception to this prior bad acts rule, which is that prior bad acts cannot be used against a Consumer if they occurred without her fault, and are unlikely to re-occur. For example, if a Consumer committed bad acts while experiencing a first-time break with reality and had no prior symptoms that led her to treatment, or if a Consumer lacked the ability to access treatment, and she now consistently avoids bad acts by obtaining medical treatment and complying with it, the use of her prior bad acts as a reason to deny her housing or employment would likely be illegal.

Conclusion

It is every bit as cruel to invidiously discriminate against mentally ill persons as it is to invidiously discriminate against physically ill persons or any others with immutable characteristics. The law recognizes this and makes this discrimination illegal.

At the same time, however, Consumers have the same obligations as other tenants and employees, albeit with the right to reasonable accommodations needed by them.

There is far more that can be learned on the subjects of housing and employment for Consumers, but the basic rules in this chapter should be known by Consumers and Supporters. Consumers have legal rights to protect them. Not only must Consumers and their Supporters know of these rights, they also must understand why they exist so that they will assert these rights when necessary and not tolerate violations of them.

CHAPTER 13

STRATEGIES FOR DEALING WITH RECALCITRANT AUTHORITIES

Introduction

Developing strategies to deal with authorities might seem to be beyond the scope of understanding laws and legal processes relative to mental illness. Strategies, however, can eliminate the need to engage in expensive and time-consuming legal procedures, and thus can be quite important when exercising legal rights.

We know that the skills and motivations of individual authorities differ. There is a spectrum among authorities, between those at the high end who go all out and those at the low end who bother themselves as little as possible. The high enders are the professionals who take their jobs seriously, who care, and who understand the importance of interacting with Supporters and appropriately welcome it. The second group, at the bottom end of the spectrum, is comprised of those who may be lacking the tools needed to do their job or are feeling overwhelmed by dealing with multiple cases of mental illness while possibly faced with stresses in their private lives too, and who have decided that communication with Supporters is unnecessary or futile.

The only strategy Supporters need for dealing with those who care and want to communicate with them is to respect their needs and burden them as little as possible. For those at the lower end of the spectrum who do not treasure input from Supporters, there are myriad strategies.

Some Strategies

Different Supporters try different strategies to effectively deal with those who are overwhelmed, who don't care, or who might view Supporters as interlopers. These strategies, all of which contain the element of persistence, include 1) giving authorities enough personal information to get them to care; 2) showing interest in the individual authorities themselves and what they are doing; 3) informing authorities clearly of the legal and moral rights of a Consumer and of her Supporter, and of the legal and moral obligations of the authorities; and 4) trying to get help from others, such as a co-worker, supervisor, or department head. A consideration of each of these strategies follows.

Strategy 1: Give authorities enough personal information to get them to care

People tend to care about others when there is a personal relationship, or when another's interests and needs are understood. People are more apt to help someone they know, someone they understand, someone for whom they can more easily feel empathy, than they are to help a stranger. One with authority and the ability to help others, a person who perhaps is given the responsibility to help others, probably shouldn't need a personal relationship with a Supporter or her loved one to be of assistance to her. But the reality often is that authorities are overworked, maybe tired, even weary, and there may be times when they would like to avoid dealing with a situation that looks to be a difficult one. This is said not as a defense for behavior that might be indefensible, but as an explanation for it. It is a reality, and because of it Supporters may need to give authorities a reason or two to help them instead of avoiding them. In this situation it is important for a Supporter to make sure that she and the Consumer she is trying to help are personalized in the authorities' minds. It isn't so much that authorities must be made to like Supporters and Consumers – some of us are more or less likeable than others – but it can be helpful if authorities know and understand us. What can be done to make this happen?

Frequently it works to talk up the good qualities of a Consumer. We don't need to wait for a specific opportunity, just slip it into conversation. Let the authorities know that our Consumer is usually, or even just occasionally, kind and generous and polite, but that when her illness takes over she becomes a different person. If she is generally or occasionally loving, let them know that, and let them know she is loved. Insert a bit of her good history as well as whatever difficulties brought her to her present situation. Make the authorities aware that with the kind of professional help they can provide, her illness and its present symptoms can recede. Remind them of how important their potential actions can be to someone who is cared about, and to the persons who care about her, and let them draw the conclusion that they too should care.

Strategy 2:   Show interest in the authorities and what they are doing

This simply means we recognize authorities as individuals with needs like the rest of us. If someone is sour or harsh to us, or is uncooperative, we might react in defensive or hostile ways. That is a reaction not uncommon for one who has been disrespected. But we aren't required to react this way. We could keep our upset to ourselves, or maybe not even get upset. Our present feelings are not the primary issue after all. Maybe we should ignore slights, at least for the time being. Certainly, we are not obliged to treat any bad words or attitudes directed toward us as personal attacks, and we are likely making a mistake if we do take them personally, since almost surely, they have nothing to do with us.

Life is hard for authorities too. When one is less than forthcoming with us, or unkind, a kind word or two from us can go a long way. "It looks like you too might be having a rough day," or "you seem a little stressed too," or "you have a pretty tough job" are easy words to offer, and they could make the person you're dealing with, who looks like she is going to make things difficult, soften a bit, open up a bit, take a keener interest in our Consumer. Of course, it might have no effect whatsoever, but a good rule of thumb to follow is that seldom is anything lost by trying. Sometimes this strategy can take on an amusingly ironic bent, where the authority a Supporter goes to for help ends up turning to the Supporter for help with her problems! More often than not, though, when a Supporter shows some interest in an authority, the authority will appreciate it, will agree with the assessment of her as being required to deal with difficult situations, will be apt to appropriately see the Supporter as a caring person who is worthy of her cooperation, and will appropriately realize that she needs to get to work on the Consumer's case and include the Supporter in the process.

It doesn't take a degree in psychology or even a lesson in manners for us to do this. It just takes an awareness of the human condition, and that no matter how anxious we might be, no matter how awful our situation is, we are not alone in experiencing distress or in being innocent victims. Everybody has something in their lives they have to deal with, and although we might feel at any moment that we suffer alone, the reality is otherwise. We can show others our interest and our concern for them, as we want them to do for us, and this can often lead to a mutually satisfying experience.

Timing can be an issue here. Sometimes an authority is facing other stresses or deadlines that will be gone tomorrow. If we determine that our communication with an authority can wait, then an important part of the strategy should be to recognize that the authority could be too busy at the moment to talk. We can then choose to talk with her later, possibly the next day. That is showing an interest in her without even communicating it, and it might make all the difference.

Strategy 3: Inform authorities clearly of our legal and moral rights and the authorities' legal and moral obligations

Strategies 1 and 2 might need supplementation. It is a good table setter to try to make an authority aware of whom we are and whom our Consumer is, and show the authority that we care about our Consumer and about the authority too. It might get the authority to want to assist us. But if assistance is not forthcoming, then it might be necessary to clearly and firmly explain what our rights are and what the authority's obligations are to us and to our Consumer.

Possibly the authority needs to be reminded of her responsibility for the Consumer's well-being, that failing to communicate might be putting the Consumer at risk, and (if all else fails) that the authority will be held legally responsible should anything bad happen to the Consumer. This is not necessarily an empty warning, certainly not with a medical provider, who has authority to disclose medical information if the provider believes it is necessary to prevent or reduce a serious and imminent threat to the health or safety of a Consumer or the public. (See Chapter 1.)

Again, when a Consumer is incapacitated to the extent that she will not authorize a disclosure of information, a medical provider may choose to disclose information which the provider determines to be in the Consumer's best interests. We should show the provider why an information disclosure to us is relevant to the Consumer's medical care. Let the authority know we believe she is authorized and perhaps obligated to disclose information, and (if necessary) that she will be responsible for a bad consequence resulting from a failure to cooperate with us. Advising her of an intent to hold her responsible can be a bit tricky, and this should be exercised with great caution and surely only as a last resort, for frequently the consequences of someone feeling threatened is either to defend their position or to detach from the conflict, neither of which will help our cause.

One fixed rule for us to follow is that when we are informing someone of her legal obligations and the consequences of violating them, there is virtually no chance of it being effective unless we do it politely.

Strategy 4: Try to get help from another person

There are going to be times when authorities won't communicate with us, and we have exhausted our attempts to make this happen. What is left is to find someone else, possibly someone with authority over the recalcitrant authority with whom we have been dealing. Try communicating with a co-worker, or find out who the authorities answer to, and contact that person. Call the other persons, or write to them, or do both. Explain help is needed and the person charged with helping is not helping. Supervisors and managers often know who their troublesome employees are, as they deal with them regularly, and possibly this complaint will not be the first one received. Give them an opportunity to supervise and manage effectively.

Summary of Strategies

We can help ourselves if we personalize our Consumer, personalize the authority, know the law, and try a different authority when one is needed.

We should be aware that we are not alone if we are dealing with less than helpful authorities, and that we have a normally functioning emotional state if we find our interactions infuriating. The burden of dealing with mental illness should be burden enough for any person's life, and in a kinder and more efficient universe Supporters would not have to devise strategies to get authorities to do their jobs. In our less than perfect world Supporters are sometimes confronted with resistance and become exasperated, at which point we find ourselves in vulnerable positions, ones where we can easily become discouraged and irritated, sometimes incensed, even to the point of rage. Frequently we are strained to maximum limits, and we can easily lose it. Feeling and expressing anger can sometimes be an effective way to let those who infuriate us beyond the breaking point understand that they are contributing to frustration and upset, or even to induce action by those who don't want to deal with an angry Supporter. But acting out our anger is never going to be the optimal way of dealing with a situation.

Supporters need to avoid directing an attack on an authority whose help is needed. Again, when people feel they are being attacked they tend to defend themselves by running away or fighting back, and neither of those things would result in help for a Consumer. It is okay for a Supporter to let an authority know she is exasperated and upset. Let her see righteous anger, let her know someone cares about the Consumer and has an emotional stake in her well-being. Let an authority know she holds the power to reduce our distress, and in essence invite her to exercise that power. But be aware that expressing anger is like walking a tightrope and falling off comes from using one wrong word or one wrong gesture or one extra decibel. Best if possible for us to play it cool, and if that isn't possible, then it is probably best to ask someone else to substitute in for us.

Situations Where Strategies Seemingly Do Not Exist

As discussed in Chapter 2, one can be committed to a locked facility for up to 72 hours if she is believed to have a mental disorder which results in her being a danger to herself or others, or which results in her being gravely disabled. There are times when we are certain of the need for this 72-hour hold, yet the authorities will not order it.

As more fully discussed in Chapter 2, one can be deemed to constitute a danger to herself or others when she expresses a desire and intention to commit imminent harm, or if there is other evidence of that desire and intention. To be deemed a danger to herself, overt statements or actions regarding suicide are not necessarily required; if one's disregard for her own safety is at the point where a serious physical injury to her is imminent, *i.e.*, she has actually placed herself in physical jeopardy, that is sufficient to qualify as being a danger to herself.

Also, as more fully discussed in Chapter 2, in order for someone to be gravely disabled she must be found to be suffering from a mental disorder which renders her unable to provide for her basic personal needs for food, clothing, or shelter.

When we see our Consumer decompensating and in dire need of hospitalization and treatment, and we know at a minimum she meets the standard of being gravely disabled, and maybe is a danger to herself or others too, we can find ourselves in the position of trying to persuade medical personnel to place an involuntary hold on her. The reason why a hold has not been ordered may have nothing to do with an authority being recalcitrant; the reason may be that there are no beds available in a locked psychiatric facility. If there is no room anywhere for our Consumer, then there is no strategy that could conceivably help. If there is nowhere to take her – which is frequently the case in many large cities – then we won't be able to convince a physician to place a hold on her; in fact, the physician might already be convinced.

There is an option that exists, although the propriety of it may not co-exist with it. If we were to take our Consumer to an emergency room in another city or county where there were beds available, that might solve the problem. Of course, that would require 1) our willingness to do this; 2) our Consumer's willingness to go with us; and 3) the medical personnel in the other city or county finding our explanation for being there acceptable.

Our willingness to do this might be induced by our desperation, but we would also need a state of mind that finds nothing wrong with this, or at least not enough wrong with it to outweigh the potential benefits. If our Consumer needs hospitalization, and if this is the only way to get it, and if the hospital with an available bed for her would profit from her admission, then maybe it would be the right thing to do.

That our Consumer in this situation would voluntarily go to a medical facility anywhere is far from a sure thing, and her willingness might have to be obtained through subterfuge. If she is feeling suicidal, and wants help, then her cooperation is pretty much guaranteed. But if she is in the midst of a psychotic break from reality, then we can't expect her cooperation. Deception might be needed, and we might be willing to provide it. But we would need to recognize the downside of using a ploy on our Consumer, which is that it could easily destroy trust. It is virtually never a good idea to deceive people; it is usually a horrible idea to deceive one prone to paranoia.

Even if we get our Consumer to an out of city or county hospital, it isn't likely that a physician would accept whatever reason we give for being at her facility. Really, the only way this arrangement could work is if the physician concluded that it didn't matter why we there, and that our Consumer's condition required a hospital admission regardless of our actions.

Taking our Consumer to another locale, one that previously had no connection to our life or our Consumer's life, in order to get her involuntarily admitted to a psychiatric facility, is all a bit of a fantastic longshot, and probably not encompassing admirable conduct by us. But possibly it is a feasible strategy and under desperate circumstances a good idea. Perhaps, though, it would be a better strategy not to wait for an emergency to arise, and instead to currently devote our available time, energy and money to persuading legislators to expand the services available for those suffering acute mental illness so that a bed will exist when one is needed.

Conclusion

There are going to be times when strategies are needed to get authorities to do what they need to do. The strategies suggested in this chapter should work at least some of the time, but they are not foolproof and likely won't work all of the time. Some will surely be more appropriate for some situations than others will be. Certainly, discretion is required before employing any of the suggested strategies. But discretion is not timidity, and timidity likely won't help our Consumer. Nothing will help her if it isn't tried, so it is probably best to try out a strategy or two. Best to be bold.

AFTERWORD

As Supporters, one of our goals is to maximize the assistance we can provide our Consumers. Knowledge of laws and how they operate, and of available programs for Consumers, will keep us in an optimal position to deal with legal issues, and to help as best we can.

Yet while a good understanding of laws and legal procedures is necessary, the help we give may still be limited. Just as we have learned to accept that there is no cure for a severe mental illness, we need to understand that sometimes there may be no way to take advantage of laws or programs, or to resolve a particular legal issue.

In order to acquire available benefits and assistance we might need to hire attorneys to navigate the system or to obtain court orders, and even then, if a Consumer is intent on obstructing attempts at assistance, she may well thwart our efforts. All of the knowledge in the world might not enable us to get benefits and assistance for a person with a severe mental illness if her symptoms include a resistance to accept help.

Sometimes it is the persons administering laws who are a greater impediment to our efforts than any limitations which might exist in those laws. Occasionally we encounter employees of agencies and businesses who seem as though they are trying to block our efforts. Maybe they feel that we are actively trying to exploit an illness, and that it is unfair for persons to be able to receive benefits not available to others merely because they are ill. Maybe they need someone over whom they can exert control so as to make themselves feel more important. Maybe they are dull or lazy. Maybe something else. We may never succeed with these people while they stand in our way, so we must devise practical approaches to get around them.

For a parent, often the very best thing that can be said to someone whose assistance is needed and who is disinclined to give it, is something like this: "My child needs help. She is innocent, she is vulnerable, and she can't help herself. So, I am trying to help her." It is a simple, accurate, strong, and often irresistible message. It should move most people. It is the unspoken message I receive every time I talk to a parent of a Consumer. Sometimes, with some people, it needs to be said directly, out loud.

Some wise person once remarked that a major difference between those who succeed and those who don't is persistence. With that in mind we need to keep at it, and we need to know this: when we are caring for a Consumer, there is no one in this world displaying a greater mixture of courage and decency than we are. Whether we are acting due to love, or due to a sense of duty, or to a combination of them, we are doing things no rational person would ever voluntarily choose to do if a reasonable alternative existed. That is a fantastically complimentary statement about us, it is something we should be proud of, and it should keep us going if nothing else will.

Sometimes we do get worn down and weakened, when we feel as if we have hit the wall and all we want to do is cry or scream. On these occasions it is good to try to keep in mind another way of perceiving our situation. Instead of focusing on our exasperation, perhaps we should pay attention to the fact that while it is overwhelmingly difficult to deal with the mental illness of someone we have a special relationship with, we are, in fact, doing this overwhelmingly difficult job. Unlike so many people whose simpler lives contain so much that is trivial or superficial – a type of life we tend to often wish for – each of us is someone who makes life better for someone else, and therefore each of us is someone who has achieved a status of importance, someone whose life has a significance, someone whose life is worth living.

Respite is necessary. It's good to take a break, so we can maintain our perspective and our sanity, and then be able to get back out there refreshed and ready to roll, to do what the situation and its limitations, including our personal limitations, allow us to do.

Of course, we will do what is in our power to do, and hopefully we will recognize that there are things beyond our power to do. We should never forget or ignore how valuable we are, nor the eminent position we have achieved, nor the myriad opportunities we have to enjoy our role. These are, after all, returns on our investments, and we have earned them.

CPSIA information can be obtained
at www.ICGtesting.com
Printed in the USA
FSHW020055230921
84954FS